Capitalism Works

Insula Qui

Table of Contents

Socialist Critiques:
1. Marketing
2. Real Estate
3. Investing
4. Banking
5. Exploitation
6. Capital Accumulation

Anarchist Critiques:
1. Freedom
2. Imperialism
3. Statism
4. Property
5. Commodity Production
6. Bosses

Progressive Critiques:
1. Inequality
2. Poverty
3. Conservationism
4. Democracy
5. Institutional Discrimination
6. Healthcare

Conservative Critiques:

1. Culture
2. Security
3. Nationalism
4. Selfishness
5. Organizational Chaos
6. Globalization

Economic Critiques:

1. Irrationality and Knowledge
2. Instability
3. Sustainability
4. Market Failure
5. Public Goods
6. Monopoly

Introduction

The aim of this book is to combat those who think capitalism cannot work. They may be ruthless radicals or simply have an imaginary boundary past which it becomes impossible to conceptualize the market economy. It is not a systematic treatise and it is not meant to be read as such, every chapter in the book is an essay in itself. This also means there is an unusual amount of repetition[1] as the book was not written in a chronological order. However, I still hope you enjoy "Capitalism Works" even despite how the form it takes may be less convenient than a cohesive work of theory.

I still do not have an editor and everything within this book is exclusively my own fault, however, I do hope that it is sufficiently pleasant to read and that the grammar is at least passable. Furthermore, some of the arguments in some chapters are less strong than they could be and unrefined, if I had gotten stuck on refining arguments at a detriment to writing the book, there would be no book. To combat most of these weaknesses two things need to be said. This is not an academic work and is not meant to be taken in an academic context, by using a systematic and methodological framework it is easy to beat many of the arguments. However, the strength of this book lies in the ability to provide many arguments from many angles, most of which are unconventional and cannot be countered by referring to some

---

[1] This is only a significant issue in the chapter "Capital Accumulation". I address it in more detail in the footnotes of that chapter.

commonly known thinker. I cannot promise that any of these arguments are conclusive, however, I can promise that these arguments will force even the least self-conscious individuals into thinking.

Important Notice

Throughout the work there are four things that may seem confusing to a right-wing libertarian audience, these are the concepts of left-wing anarchism, right-wing liberalism, conservatism as against the free market and market socialism. Left-wing anarchism has been the mainstream of anarchism for the entire existence of anarchism as a philosophy. When I use the term anarchism I am referring exclusively to left-wing anarchism, if I am referring to "anarcho"-capitalism, I will classify that I am doing so. Left-wing anarchism is against private property and advocates for a violent insurrection that will result in a society where there is no inequality. It differs from regular socialism as the anarchists do not believe that the state is a functional means of achieving socialism. Usually, anarchists also believe in democratic decision making, however only outside the bourgeoisie democracy of the liberal state.

Liberalism, as a tradition, evolved into three distinct modern political positions. The first is the form of libertarianism promoted by the followers of Mises and Hayek, the second is the sort of neo-liberalism shared between the right wing of the US democratic party and conservative think tanks. Only the third form of liberal philosophy is what we may imagine as liberalism, this is the social liberal position. This is where conservative think tanks and democrats differ they both accept free enterprise and the market as useful, however, the democrats are also liberals in the social sense. Social liberalism tends to emphasise the social problems of inequality and marginalization as the basis for a free and liberal society. Often when I refer to liberalism, I refer to the originary philosophy that spawned these three distinct directions, but do exercise discretion.

In Europe conservatives are not free market fundamentalists, this is because conservatism does not have a foothold in Jeffersonian tradition. There is no distinct strain of economic liberalism in conservatism in the non-American world. In my section criticizing conservatives, I am mainly dealing with conservative positions without Jeffersonian politics as an originary principle.

When it comes to market socialism, anyone who does not know how it functions is rightfully befuddled. The basic idea of it is that workers should run all businesses without having bosses and without having hierarchy. Thus market socialism can retain the price system, individual incentive and everything else the market has to offer. This is, of course, a flawed theory, but it does not suffer from internal contradiction, socialism does not need to be synonymous with central planning. And since a lot of arguments would become about central planning if I did not discount that possibility, and since every libertarian under the sun already knows the flaws of central planning, I use this concept to strengthen my arguments. I do go over problems of central planning and delve into a deeper discussion in the chapter on instability. The strong arguments also include showing how central planning becomes the only alternative for the market with the implication that market economies are preferable to centrally planned ones.

Socialist Critiques

I – Marketing

Socialists often claim that a great evil in capitalism is how the market economy allocates money for things that don't have real usable value. The prime example for this is marketing, which socialists further use to enforce their notion that capitalism causes false desires. No one with an intellectual spirit likes advertisements so the socialists play into an emotional issue to boot. Furthermore, this is an issue the anti-capitalists can use to get sympathy from traditionalists who care about culture. What is a greater subversion of culture than an economy built on creating false desires for meaningless products using an empty, worthless medium of advertising? This is a perfect storm of relatability and seemingly correct reasoning to fool the vast majority who are unprepared when they come into contact with anti-marketing rhetoric.

This makes defending advertising a daunting task, marketing is seen as exploitative, wasteful, decadent and to top it off, personally inconvenient. How could it possibly be good and proper to blast people with messages telling them to buy various material objects? This seems like an obvious reason for why capitalism is an unethical system and should not be allowed to exist. And the critics of capitalism have a point, advertising really is designed, at least in part, to form a corporate culture and control people's spending, it may seem as if they are right on both an emotional and empirical standpoint. The task becomes seemingly impossible only after a casual glance.

However, what we need to keep in mind is that advertising is not meant for intellectuals but rather the individuals in society who will go along with all possible trends. The sort of people who do not make decisions based on careful research. And this is the great majority of people, this is who advertising is useful for. Sure, advertisements can convince average people to want to buy brands they previously had not bought, but advertisement cannot make anyone want material goods that they have no use for. The only thing that can make a person want to purchase something is the person with unsatisfied needs and money to spend. It may be the case that societal wealth will make people desire increasingly more useless things and advertising can point shallow people to useless products that have no real value, but the desire itself is incited by the individual and not the advertisement. If people who want to consume products that they think they will enjoy, they will derive value from advertising. Seeing marketing campaigns or targeted advertisements can point consumers towards novel products, facilitating innovation in the free market. This also means that people who want shallow things will get advertised to as there is a potential profit for advertising to shallow people.

And, of course, advertisements will use human instincts and urges to show how the advertised product may benefit the life of the potential customer since the customer aims to fill some inner want with the product. No one would want to buy a product if the people using that product are depicted as miserable failures. The advertisement may misrepresent the degree of utility derived but it must represent the desirable utility. If people want to look more beautiful and if an advertisement promises to make them look better upon using their product, they will use the advertised product to improve their appearance. The people chosen to market that product must also be beautiful people, as if a beauty product made a person less attractive, it would not fill the desire to become more attractive. Most people would still have previously had the urge to increase their personal beauty without being subjected to advertising. But those who want to increase their own aesthetic value are just directed towards one particular brand by the advertisement.

Any remaining illusion about advertising making people want undesirable things should be shattered when we discover that useless purchases are just the result of a vast amount of civilizational wealth. People are able to spend their money on useless products as people have more money than they know what to do with. The same simple-minded people who fall into the trap of advertising are the same people who are taught by our culture and education that they should be constantly spending money. Modern consumers with a vast excess of money have no ability to hang onto their money, they have no desire to save any money but rather desire to spend as much as possible. Thus the advertisers can capture this facet of the culture of the contemporary West and profit from it. But the advertisers are not to blame as they did not create our culture. In a sense, advertising is a reflection of the lowest form of any culture, it shines a light pointing towards all of the decay that our civilization suffers. Advertising is the medium that most plainly appeals to the lowest common denominator.

And this makes it really easy to hate advertisements. How could you not, considering that advertisements are simply profiting off our failures as a society. If we, as a society, had not failed then we would not see advertisements of the magnitude they take and we would not see advertisements that pander to the worst of us. For more sensitive people, this can induce despair and disgust, but for the aforementioned commoners, advertisements are just useful information. Thus, we may try to cover the issue up by hiding the advertising and not facing the fact that we have a civilizational issue. However, this would only have negative effects since it means that those without higher sensibilities lack the information they previously had and will make even worse decisions.

Furthermore, for a very low cost, projects can obtain funding just by using advertisements. In the modern economy, it is a viable strategy to forsake investors and seize control over your own products by using advertisements to fund them. It only imposes an inconvenience on the person who gets a product for free or extremely cheap thanks to the value of mass advertising. And no one can even compel any person to pay attention to advertisements, all forms of marketing are easily ignorable in almost any context. The only price is a few moments of boredom during commercial breaks or a tiny amount of clutter on websites, which any adult human should know how to cope with. And it is true that there are billions of dollars spent on advertising and market research, but this only demonstrates the effectiveness of advertising, if it was unable to generate sales and to allocate resources, money would not be spent in advertising. If advertising was a psychological trick that made people buy things that they did not want, most money would be spent on advertising to the detriment of production, which is not the truth. Furthermore, the importance of market research shows that advertising by itself is at least insufficient of making consumers want useless products. What we can infer is that advertising is simply spreading information to people incapable of doing deeper research in a flashy and loud manner.

However, all firms must advertise to a degree if they want to find success and as such there will be a degree of wide-reaching marketing costs in an economy. This is solely because when no one is aware that a product exists, no one can buy that product. Thus it must be true that on some level advertising helps people make decisions, but this could theoretically be optimized. For example, instead of advertising, there could be government experts supporting certain products or worker councils checking quality and price. These would probably be far less costly methods of figuring out which products people should use as they are not multi-billion dollar industries and require far less funding. This seems rational at its face value but this doesn't mean that it has to go contrary to advertising. If the optimal way of spreading information regarding products is to form independent entities of experts, the people who have a problem with advertising should work more on assembling the councils of technocrats. They would quickly make advertising obsolete as it would no longer be profitable if people listened to the advice of technocrats instead of any corporate marketing. Since advertising has not yet been obsoleted, we can only assume that people prefer advertisements over the objective consumer-oriented advice of pro-worker groups.

There is one final argument to be made, it could be that advertising is a symptom of needless parallelism in capitalism. Since companies are putting their resources into defeating one another, the enterprises are unable to advance production. All the resources spent on advertising are resources not spent on producing material goods. This again seems compelling, if companies weren't trying to wrest capital away from one another and their own workers, then they could focus on the actual advancement of the economy. However, since economic competition facilitates advertising, companies have to spend money that could otherwise have been put to good use. This seems like a giant waste that would be avoided were it not for advertising.

But another problem arises here, this argument does not make the case for socialism. As said before, advertising is simply the cultural manifestation of the least intelligent in a society, namely the people who supposedly fall for advertisements. This means that the argument proposed isn't an argument that logically infers socialism, but rather an argument that encourages the creation of a strong culture which is able to shield people against using advertisements as their guide to purchasing products. If we reached a state where our culture could produce alternative methods of earning money and spreading information, we would not need any advertising. The way to make this possible is through education, strong communities and traditional, anti-materialist cultural values. A socialistic economy could abolish marketing, but it would also bring about socialism. The question we have to ask ourselves here is if socialism is inherently good or bad and not a question about marketing. The issue of marketing becomes null when we are presented with alternative non-socialist ways of doing away with marketing if it truly produces no value. If we would rather not put our own effort into lifting up those with a low station and delegate this to the state, we can now rest assured that socialism is the only way. If we actually do care for the workers we would obviously be overjoyed at finding this easy solution to marketing without the need for socialism.

And this is not to forget that some of the most disastrous and corrupt advertising is government propaganda, something which is often present in socialist countries. Even though some might contend that socialist countries can't exist as they are oxymoronic, we can see countries who collectivize the means of production use propaganda in one form or another to cement their control over the body politic. And this is simply another form of marketing, but a marketing of the state, the party and not the marketing of any product that people actually desire.

And furthermore, this ignores the productive side of marketing which is the research that goes into advertisements. Companies need to determine who their product appeals to and how they can sell their product to the group of people who want their product. Thus, advertising creates a more thorough understanding of the market and of the people involved in the market. This information is often publicized to a certain extent and helps all participants in the market make better decisions with an increased awareness of the conditions in the market economy. Marketers allow everyone who wants to set up a business to know how to make products that people want and which would also be cost-effective to produce. In this manner, there is a great wealth of information derived from advertising that can be used to create a more efficient economy and increase the level of awareness for each individual who wants to sell a product.

II – Real Estate

From devoted marxists to georgists, socialists love to act as if real estate was something inherently corrupt or useless, this comes from a general misunderstanding of the purpose of real estate. It is fashionable among these circles to say that land should belong to everyone and that taking land as property is inherently wrong, therefore what is even more wrong is profiting from the land that one takes as property in the real estate industry. The gains from real estate are seen as completely fictitious and a detriment to the society. It is assumed that it would be much more humane if there was no inherent economic profit from real estate.

Usually, the abolition of real estate means that the land owned privately should instead be seized and allocated by communities or the state for the supposed profit of everyone. Or that the profits earned from the use of land should be taxed so heavily as to make them mostly irrelevant. Furthermore, some socialists advocate for a decentralized seizing of land and doing away with allocation altogether, allowing people to come and go as they wish and set themselves up on any unoccupied land. The last of these is just an anarchist fantasy and would result in such an immense amount of chaos that it's not even worthwhile to discuss it. When there is no order for the allocation of land, that land will be allocated to random persons and not in any rational way. Thus both economic decisions and personal decisions become impossible.

The real debate then becomes whether the allocation of land should be decentralized and for profit or centralized with no profit involved. The other debate to be had is if land can even be owned, can any person even claim that they have a right to any land at all? We could discount both of these ideas by saying that the government is corrupt and profit motives are good, but that is a cop out and we need to use other arguments when it comes to the topic of land use. Land is a completely unique economic issue and it may be the case that even if the market is completely free, it should still not have the current structure of land use structure. Thus, we must consider another perspective added to the debate, that land use should be decentralized and not for profit.

The first topic is simple to address when land use is delegated to people who themselves will not utilize it, there will be some systemic inefficiency as they have no reason to use that land properly. Furthermore, even if the delegates who manage land wanted to maximize the value of land, they would have no way of knowing how to do so without becoming, in essence, private owners of that land. However, if we structured property rights in a way that people can submit their own claims to certain parcels of land, it seems as if we can fix this issue. If people can submit their claims to land to these central agencies based on the public good, these agencies could then allocate the land in a way that is supposedly in the best interest of the public. After all, this is similar to what happens currently with zoning laws. And we can here even assume that this land-allocation is democratic to avoid the problem of personal power. It seems as if abolishing profit would decidedly be better than any other system of allocating land. The people would have their overarching interests respected and the land will be allocated in such a way that the society as a whole is happy with, no one person's narrow interests will get in the way of what is good for the people as a whole.

This remains true until we consider the situation where there are people with their own personal interests who require access to certain areas. What happens when the council will not approve a project that someone has a stake in? You can say that capitalism also prevents access to land due to monetizing land use, but this is unfair. When people have the ability to demonstrate their necessity for this land, they can obtain loans and investors and thus become able to appropriate that land. All of the profit-seeking capitalist parties do this out of their own interest and have that interest directly tied to the maintenance of that land. If the capitalists lacked this intimate interest, then they may make much worse decisions than if there is a private connection to the land. The owners and loaners take the responsibility for any misuse of land as they all have a partial stake in the land. Any centralized entity is unable to have a personal interest in ensuring that land is well-ordered and thus will only create a system where land is distributed haphazardly.

There is no way to obtain loans and purchase land under socialism, one can only hope that the central planner has mercy on them. Convincing the party official is much harder than convincing enough people to procure necessary funds. In theory, this may be for the good of the supposed social interest, but individually and practically, this means that no matter who can expect to benefit from the land, they have no access to it. Unless they can present a use for the land that is not only gainful but also popular. Unglamorous uses of land would become too scarce to provide for unglamorous needs.

This system may be useful in some circumstances, but will by necessity result in an overproduction of certain goods and an underproduction of others as individuals are choked by the force of the collective. This is because private people cannot use land for productive enterprise unless they first obtain the consent of the socialist council. An individual also has no way to demonstrate how productive that enterprise would be under socialism. If there is no price system and no market, the only way to determine the good an enterprise does is through trial and error. As such a person cannot start any venture without the risk being accepted by the general public. Since both risks and benefits are socialized, we must see a general drop in production as there are no interest groups who benefit more from starting enterprises.

This is with the exception of the people who want to use the democratic system of land allocation for their own personal benefit at a cost to the rest of society. This generally means that individuals both cannot and will not create productive ventures as they are locked out of the use of land that they need to start their enterprise. Decision making in the economy will slow down tremendously and the economy will stop producing as much as what was previously produced. This will be present in every industry that requires the use of any land and not just isolated to land-intensive industries.

Even though there may be a utopian ideal of full automation which would drastically alleviate all of the aforementioned problems, the sort of economy where land use is democratic cannot produce many luxury items or niche products. This must be true as there is no interest in allocating land to less widespread purposes when uses that coincide with the general interest are more universal. However, all people belong to very specific groups and have their niche interests, thus everyone would lose access to goods they otherwise would have had a use for. If the allocation of the land was done for the common good and not solely by individual initative the land will only produce common goods. The one solution to this is a form of market socialism where worker-lead businesses transact on the free market without the involvement of the capitalist, this is the option of a decentralized profitless system I mentioned above.

In this system individual worker collectives would claim unoccupied land and create their own enterprises, this makes the problem of land allocation mostly vanish as individual enterprise is still highly valued. Furthermore, everyone who wants to create a business can do so freely as long as there is unoccupied land and as long as the entrepreneurial workers can then use that land for whatever purpose they wish. But here we run into another problem, these workers need to be clothed and fed while they are setting up their own enterprise. The workers cannot enlist capitalists or investors filling the purpose of capitalists, thus they need to fund themselves. One solution to is to either force entire worker collectives to stake their own money on every new enterprise. But this approach would be a giant risk diffused among all the labourers in a collective and not only a singular capitalist and his investors. It is not unreasonable to say that socializing risks among workers will cause less innovation as workers need to put their well-being on the line to create any market ventures. The capitalist can solve this problem by providing resources to workers while he doesn't make any profits and only recoup what he spent after the business has been successful for many years.

Or it is possible to imagine a system where these projects are funded or deemed worthy by something akin to the banking system, but based on socialist principles. In this case, there are two options, first, the "socialist banks" become another capitalist class as they hold the power over the capital in the economy and thus create another system that goes contrary to socialism. This would result in worker exploitation by these agents that are supposed to help the workers as they provide resources for the functioning of all enterprises and they will not do so out of plain charity. Wherever there is a potential for fulfilling self-interest, it is more beneficial for anyone to do so than to not. The other option is to have the society decide which projects are worthwhile and then take the risk that would have been assumed by the bank entity. This causes the problems already described and will create a halt in business activity due to the troubles involved with a social allocation of resources instead of a private one.

Furthermore, the worker exploitation by socialistic banks must be, by necessity, worse than worker exploitation by regular banks. Regular banks concentrate their efforts, in large part, towards "exploiting" the capitalist class and not towards the working class. The capitalist class is the most profitable subject for the bankers. The socialist banks must focus entirely on workers and as such the forces that otherwise would have gone to profiting from capitalists will go to profiting from workers. If there is no chance to profit institutionally, these bankers will profit by personally gaining more power through their bank. Although the establishment of socialist banks is a far better scenario than the other forms of socialism presented, it is still suboptimal when compared to capitalism.

Another thing we need to address is the real estate industry as it stands right now and the problems socialists have with the shape of real estate in capitalism. The most pressing issue is probably the fact that it seems that land speculation can create gains from processes that do not add any value to anyone. One can buy land and sell it at a premium without themselves contributing to the quality of the land and only profiting from either the stupidity of the buyer or the inherently corrupt system. This approach is also fundamentally flawed. It ignores the important role that land allocation plays in any economy and we can demonstrate how buying and selling what amount to pieces of paper that denote ownership of land does actually create value.

This may seem absurd at first as many things in the modern economy do. This is because legal processes are further removed from their original purpose, but it is important to determine that land is owned by people who can take the best use of it as discussed above. The people who buy and sell these empty scraps of paper perform a vital social role by assuming the risk of holding that property. And they do even more than that, the land speculators assume the responsibility to find the best pieces of land and charge such a price that there will be no social deficit when it comes to land, at least in all cases where social deficit can be avoided. If there was a social deficit when it comes to land, it would have many adverse effects on everyone within that society who cannot afford the losses of land scarcity. These problems can all be avoided, but it is important to keep in mind that no other system than the one of the free market can represent the scarcity of quality land in the accessibility to land. Land is scarce and also one of the most vital parts of any economy, so it must be allocated with the utmost care. If land is more accessible, it will be wasted more quickly than if it was less accessible. Most anti-capitalist solutions focus on making existing land more accessible even though that is a flawed approach at its core. There can be no elimination of the scarcity when it comes to land and land must always be allocated with the consideration that it is scarce.

The point of the real estate industry is to see the value in land and then utilize that land in a fashion that will be a social benefit. The realtors delegate this utilization of land to third parties and that is their social role. The people who produce value are the people the speculators sell the land to. If their predictions about the quality of land were right they will earn a surplus from whatever people do on that land as they will manage to charge higher prices to access that land. When someone has a valuable use for land, they are willing to pay proportionately to the value their use of land creates. As such, the speculators can focus on making the land more presentable so that the people who want to use that land would see the value the land will provide them. The realtors also must give additional information on the land, if they hope to sell that land for a high price.

The final argument is whether or not it is just and ethical to have land ownership in a society in the first place. The question of economic efficiency does not matter at all to the socialists when it comes to ethics as this is a question of morality and should be addressed using ethics and not economics. It may be useful to point out how land ownership gives a good economic incentive to take care of land, but this is irrelevant when discussing the problems of the fundamental legal systems in societies. Here, the socialists assert that no person can do something special to gain full and private ownership of land. If you occupy and use a house or work at a factory, you can own those properties to the degree to which you utilize them, but the land itself can never be owned.

It becomes improper to completely exclude anyone from any piece of land as doing so will create a system where land, which is a naturally common resource, is kept exclusively to arbitrary people. You may be allowed to own your house under socialism, but you have no right to the ground under your house. And this is not an absurd notion, there really is nothing special about staking a claim to land and then saying that you own that land, anyone could do that with any piece of land and it can quickly start to seem like land ownership is just legal fiction and not grounded in reality. But this is not how people or any other living species work.

It may be said that we should eliminate land ownership even despite the nature of man. But the argument then becomes a debate on whether ethics come from the nature of man or if ethics are solely derived from the material conditions of any given era. Included in that debate must be the assumption that proper law is based on ethics and corresponds to some degree to what people themselves perceive as proper and just. If we take the position that law does not need to correspond to what is moral, then we can make no claim about how property rights should be structured but can only argue about if property rights fit a nebulous moral standard which has no ground as it does not correspond with law.

There are strong arguments to be made for both a relativistic interpretation of ethics and a naturalistic interpretation of ethics, both of these interpretations form different conclusions when it comes to land use. With relativistic ethics, one has to argue that when there is no need for property rights in the current era of human development, then we should abolish property rights. Thus if we live in an advanced industrial society, we may be better off when we abolish the right to own land as private land use only causes problems that are completely unnecessary. When we need to reach a point of heightened comfort, it may be useful to keep property rights, but there comes a point where industry does not need to grow and property in land becomes exploitative as people have to pay for something arbitrary with no social gain derived from it. If we take ethics as something relative to the current condition of humanity we must morally concede that property needs to eventually be done away with if humans can sustain themselves for an unlimited amount of time without economic advancement.

If ethics are objective, we need to integrate the territorial nature of man into our conception of what is and what isn't ethical and since humans naturally claim the territory that they occupy, we must say that territory that is properly occupied belongs to the occupant. This can also be used to argue for other systems, but the argument necessitates that we accept property rights in land as ethically just in one way or another. Furthermore, this taken to its logical conclusion results in a form of stateless capitalism where each person has full control over their property unless they themselves have chosen to delegate managerial duties.

When arguing from the side of both purist forms of morality we are left with different daunting tasks, From one side we have to explain how humans created states over millennia if it was so contrary to human nature and how we have constantly lived under power structures while civilized. But if we want to defend the relativistic version of morality we have to somehow explain what creates the conditions that create morality in the first place and find some dialectical origin. I have seen no interpretation of relativistic ethics that can hold up under the possibility that the dialectical starting point from the current ethics is the original nature of man nor have I seen any such systems that provide better starting points for the development of a system of ethics. Thus relativistic ethics still become ultimately dependent on the original ethics based on the structure of biological human morality and the various changes in opposition to that can simply be seen as perversions of natural ethics.

And from this perspective, I would argue that we can use dialectics to demonstrate how power structures have distorted the proper ethical principles and how it would be optimal to return to the basic nature of morality without the perversions that have created different legal systems. We can utilize the dialectical method to analyze how the interests of those in power and the interests of the subjects of power have been in conflict and have created the system of law that is currently prevalent. We can then analyze different corruptions and see how the changes towards power that disrupt the proper law have had ill effects and how the dialectical movements towards lessening power have created better results. This should not be viewed through a lens of a battle between populism and elitism or as a class conflict in the marxist sense. Rather, this is a conflict between independence and dependence, a populist movement can increase dependence on power and an elitist movement can increase independence from power. The form that power takes should be irrelevant as all power is ultimately artificial. There can be no power without someone demanding to be obeyed and another person obeying. Power is a two-part relationship which is only created if both parties fall subject to the illusion of power.

Contrary to what socialists believe this view is not the conflict between the oppressed and the oppressor insofar as it relates to free market capitalism. The structure of full rights in property is the original structure of the morality of man and as such is independent from power rather than being in itself a relation of power. We can posit anthropological arguments for naturalistic socialism, but if we were to do that we would also have to realize that the anthropological structures of socialism have been manifestations of tribalism. The family has replaced the tribe and the only modern equivalent of a tribe is a local community. Thus there could be a naturalistic fascism, but which can never take the form of leftist socialism. Since property is the original nature of man and not some construct that has been established, we can see the previous conflicts as conflicts between the original nature of man and between those who seek to rule man. Or when we put it even more distinctly this becomes a conflict between those who defend property rights and those who oppose property rights. This would imply that the righteous position is in favour of property rights provided that the previous suppositions are true.

And lastly, there is the matter of some socialists claiming that all modern property was appropriated by violence and thus it is just to reappropriate it in the same way. This claim is hard to defeat as the historical evidence does show that most modern claims to property originated from centuries of war and an enclosure of common lands by the state. It seems as though we can reduce most of all land owned to some sort of originary violence or another and as such we shouldn't promote the sustained ownership of this land. This is at least if we eventually wanted to form a society with property rights that are moral and follow along with the naturalistic reasoning for ethics. This is not mentioning the thousands of ways in which indirect violence by the state has affected the structure of property ownership. It may seem tempting to give up on property in land altogether and to form a society in which there is no land ownership, but this is the opposite of a solution. What really needs to happen is that those who were wronged in any way by how property rights have been allocated should be compensated for the violations against their property. And if an ancestry can be established, those who can demonstrate wrongs to their ancestors should be able to reclaim the property that was wrongfully appropriated.

In every other case where there is no person from whom the land was demonstrably appropriated and no lineage to find the people who the land rightfully belongs to, we can simply sustain the land as is, and this is the great majority of cases. This is simply because the current residents of the land are the ones that have cultivated it and have been the most responsible for the well-being and proper management of the land. Furthermore, most large companies own their land by having abused the state for their own benefit, thus there can be a case made that the land of large companies should be confiscated and appropriated to some other parties. This is questionable.

III – Investing

Supposedly investment allows the capitalist class to retain hegemony over the economy by increasing the amount of capital concentrated in the capitalist class without ever actually increasing production. Investment must then only serve as a tool to increase the wealth of the bourgeoisie without the upper class having to increase their productivity. If this is the case, and if we assume that there is a violent oppression of the working class fundamentally based in their relation to capital, then investment will supposedly constantly increase the stranglehold the capitalists have on society. And when the capitalists can gain additional wealth from investment without personal contribution to material production, the capitalists can also exploit the working class further as they have more power on the market and not just steeper capital relations. This logic seems fairly sound for the most part, however, it relies on a contextualization that does not have a grounding in reality and makes assumptions contrary even to socialist theory.

This takes investment as a phenomenon in a vacuum and does not look for the requirements of investment and it assumes that there is an inherent class-based discrimination when it comes to investment. Furthermore, the possibility that class is determined by the same factors as the propensity to invest is ignored. This all has to do with ignoring the important factor of time preference when it comes to investment, that is the fact that people will always prefer present gratification over equivalent future gratification if all other things are equal. By adding time into our logic, we are able to establish the proper framework in which we can actually see the reason why there are class distinctions related to investment and why investment is not making money out of nothing.

We can assume the worst of the socialist examples when it comes to the nature of the bourgeoisie. This is the narrative that there is some sort of rich parent who has a child who then inherits so much wealth that the child has no theoretical need to work a day in their life. Even though this is rarely the case when it comes to the upper class and the families who have wealth usually see it decrease and increase each generation depending on the quality of heirs, we can assume this to be true. I take this to be the case in order to prevent any possible fallacious arguments for the side that I will be defending.

First, to be able to invest you need to have stores of money, this does not only mean inheriting great amounts but rather delaying gratification and not spending that money once it has been attained. Furthermore, to have the money to pass down in the first place, the capitalist class cannot only benefit from their institutional dominance but also need to maintain it. This requires performing some amount of administrative duties which these people will be compensated for resulting in their wealth. This compensation might be far too much for the use value that these people create, but it is important to note that the capitalist class cannot function solely off of investments unless they want to live on a small fraction of their wealth each year. And even if we take orthodox marxist theory at face value, someone at some time needed to create this wealth by productive activity, it cannot wholly be that capitalist wealth is completely vacuous.

This means that not only is time preference vital in investment, but also the money that is invested must have first been acquired via some degree of productive activity. Even the most devoted marxists acknowledge that in early industrial history and in building up new industries, capitalists serve a functional role as entrepreneurs. This means that the capitalist must have at some point performed the role of entrepreneur to achieve the wealth that he has at this point. This is not to say that the institutional domination by the capitalist class is necessarily a faulty thesis, but rather that it cannot fully explain why the capitalist class has wealth[2]. This means that someone at some point had to delay their own gratification to have the ability to bestow the wealth first gained by production further onto his progeny and that his progeny also have to delay gratification to maintain that wealth through investment.

It is not true that the money the capitalists have through investment is only the result of some inherent corruption in the capitalist system, but rather the wealth is gained by prioritizing future well-being over present well-being. If capitalists had not sacrificed their immediate gratification for the possibility to earn more money in the future, they would not have had the chance to invest. It takes this sort of personal sacrifice to be able to maintain wealth. Even though putting off consumption may not seem like a

---

[2] Although I have profound disagreements with marxist class theory, it is not my purpose to debate that here.

sacrifice for many, when we talk about how humans prefer to act, it cannot be considered as anything else. All people who wish to invest have to give up what they want and go against their immediate interest, this in itself constitutes a sacrifice. Thus to sustain class structures, the capitalists who are already in the dominant class must constantly sacrifice present gains in exchange for future wealth so as to maintain their class status. This means that the workers, provided they do not invest, cannot reach the capitalist class and even if they manage to attain private property, cannot sustain their wealth. It is fundamentally true that the problem is not with rich people having a hegemony through investment but rather people who invest having a hegemony on being rich. No one else can stay in the capitalist class without providing sustained attention to maintaining their wealth. This in itself is a lifestyle choice that is not appealing to many, it is perfectly reasonable to forgo wealth for the lifestyle consequences that result from it.

Furthermore, all people who are not extremely wealthy are not barred from investing if they make more money than the minimum cost of living. The poor could still hypothetically multiply their wealth with prudent investment[3] if they wanted to do so and thus ascend in the class structure, however, most people prefer the ability to enjoy the present state of life over having a better future. This is the cause of them not being rich and not that the institutions of capitalism forbid them from ascending in class. They personally

---

[3] This is primarily due to how compounding interest will eventually multiply wealth. Even 2% annual interest will double the principal in 40 years.

do not possess the qualities necessary for increasing personal wealth and as such are unable to increase their personal wealth to change their economic class.

It also does not matter how much more capital the upper class has in comparison to the lower class and a simple increase in capital cannot increase the oppression in capital relations. Rather, the structure of the capital relations is what determines the degree of oppression that the workers suffer. It is not a matter of how many are extremely wealthy or the amount of wealth they have compared to poor people. This is true within socialist theory until we assume that there is a correlation between monopoly and the station of the wealthy. The marxists now have to demonstrate in what fashion does the increase in wealth in individual rich people change the relations to capital in such a way that the workers are more oppressed There is no way to do so other than to claim that inequality in itself is oppression, and we cannot necessarily assume that increased inequality must also bring more oppressive capital relations.

And claiming that inequality is oppression is a null argument unless we are willing to resort to dubious concepts in order to back the ideology behind socialism. In traditional marxist philosophy what is important is the inherent relation between the upper class of exploiters and the lower class of the exploited. The oppression is inherent in the class relation and not in the inequality of different individuals. The class relation is not any different when the wealthy are more wealthy and the poor are poorer. Thus until class in itself is abolished, there can be no justice and the degree of inequality is not a pressing concern. This is very apparent in marxists constantly fighting against "small business fetishism".

Investment thus is unable to make the capitalist class into a dominant class when it comes to oppressing workers. If there is a class distinction between the owners of capital and those who work that capital, it does not matter how wealthy any class is. Even in basic socialist theory, the problem lies within the fact that workers are alienated from their own labour. Investment cannot sustain capital relations, no matter if there were no very rich people and even if the class distinctions were minimal, capitalism would be as oppressive due to the necessity to exploit workers to gather surplus value. This is true if we hold labour power to be constant between the two scenarios, which is a fair assumption as labour organization capitalizes on worsening conditions. This is still a very incomplete argument and there are multiple fair objections.

It can still be asserted that the rich get more out of the economy than they put in if they invest and as such the rich can use investment to further their class interest. But this falls on the problem described above, the poor also get more out of the economy than they contribute if they invest. The problem is that poor people are less willing to reduce the quality of their life. Socialists often bring out the argument that once each person's needs are met, the rest is gratuitous, so a proper socialist cannot even argue that it is basic human decency that prohibits the poor from making investments. Only from a neo-liberal standpoint can there be a proper argument for why it is bad that there is such an inequality in investment. But from a socialist standpoint, this argument is self-defeating as the economic logic used by the socialists does not account for gratuitous pleasures being valuable. No matter if the neo-marxists promote hedonism and focus on pleasure, the underlying communist philosophy defeats the argument. The leisure described by Marx is distinct from idleness, yet it seems as if idleness is the new socialist ideal.

In the western world, most workers earn above what is necessary for subsistence and do so by immense amounts, this should imply that the workers could invest a significant proportion of their earnings. If we go solely by numbers, these earnings may be very different between the rich and the poor as the rich have more of what could be described as gratuitous pleasures. But this still is not an argument against investment on the basis of it helping the rich to get more out of the economy than they put in. In a systematic fashion it would seem as if all poor and rich invested, all people would get more out of the economy. This is ridiculous as all people would themselves be the economy. This may only be countered by saying that the interest rates would rapidly decrease when the demand for credit is met, but this would also mean that the rich cannot accumulate wealth as rapidly.

It can be said that increased wealth in the capitalist class puts the working class in a worse position in negotiation as the capitalist class gains more market power and due to this the capitalist class will be in a better position. But this logic only holds true as far as the process of economic advancement causes an increase in land prices. Otherwise, if there is no increase in land prices, there is no increase in the cost of living and capitalist investment is not at the cost of the workers but mostly other capitalists. The living conditions of the workers are held stable insofar as their rent does not increase. This means that the capitalists may be able to insulate the economic growth into their own class, but it doesn't put them into a better position when it comes to the relation between capitalists and the workers except for the fact that the quality of the work that workers do is stagnant. Furthermore, this profit insulation is only possible with the involvement of the state creating the sort of institutional systems that can prohibit the working classes from reaping the value that they produce. When capital is not artificially scarce, workers do not need to be subservient to capitalists as there is more capital than there are workers. There is still the problem of infinite growth within a finite system, but that is another issue. Until all material resources have been exhausted, the workers are only subservient to capitalists as far as the state induces scarcity in capital.

Even if we accept communist premises as completely right, we cannot properly say that investment is the cause or even an important factor in capitalist class domination. As such it is not any sort of important analytical factor beyond the structure of capitalism that the communists already view as rotten. There is no cohesive argument from principles against investment from a socialist standpoint that can completely condemn investment as anything more than just additional legal fiction within the capitalist system.

Here we can arrive at another way to look at investment and this is the capitalist position, the notion that investment is responsible for economic growth and human advancement. Not only is investment not bad, investment is the sole thing that creates prosperity of the degree that we see in modern society, there are many arguments against this notion, but the argument for it is fairly simple. When capital is created, that capital will increase the value available in the economy, since the economy has more value available, there must also be an increase of prosperity in the economy. Unless that value itself is insulated in one certain class, which is fairly impossible as it is necessary to hire workers and sell products on the market, then the economic growth must benefit all members in society. We can use a historical example, that is the growth of the ownership of various things that were originally luxuries, such as refrigerators, cars, and computers, so we can demonstrate how the market system will make added capital into an improvement in the lives of everyone. The ownership of refrigerators and computers has become a common phenomenon although they were only available to the highest elites in the past. The actual economic logic behind this is too complex to explain here, but we can logically see how the growth in capital has benefited the entirety of society and it's not as if the rich have exclusive control over all increased capital.

Thus we must establish that economic growth is a thing that is positive for everyone in society and that is also desirable. This is not economic growth in the form of gross domestic product, but the increase of actuarial value in the lives of each person. Economic growth cannot be achieved without an increase in the resources available in the economy, to create new resources one must have access to wealth they can use to create capital goods. In this manner, investment and saving can provide the capital that can be used to create additional capital and thus investment is directly responsible for economic growth. We can also formulate it like this, for there to be more wealth in the future people have to undertake future-oriented projects and to do so they need patterns of money-spending that are also directed at the future.

This means that for there to be more wealth in the future, we must restrict consumption in the present so we would have the capital necessary to increase social wealth in the future. If there is no saving and if there is no investment, we can only ever have a perpetual stagnation in the economy. This will result in an economy that has resources being distributed in circular patterns without additional growth. The only argument against this logic is that technical innovation itself creates an increase in capital, however, technical research requires funding and has to be adopted, both of which are capital intensive. There is no way in which to adopt new technology without first getting the funds to innovate and then adapt the innovation.

IV – Banking

No one likes banks and socialists always jump to critiquing banks[4], for accumulating profits for the capitalist class without producing any actual value. After all, the entire banking system is playing around with numbers and creating interest for those who already have a large amount of money. Even worse, debt puts the poorest in society into a situation of debt slavery in which they are functionally forced to work for the bank and not for themselves as they are so tied to the bank. For many reasons, arguing against banking seems like a surefire way to effectively argue against capitalism. And this is why a lot of fascists have also adopted the same rhetoric, albeit with anti-semitic undertones[5]. However, the socialists are right on this one, banking really is an exploitative industry, the question is if the exploitative nature of banking necessarily reflects poorly on the market economy.

Using methods of historical and praxeological analysis we are able to conclude that banking cannot be used necessarily as a critique of capitalism in itself. The current form of the banking industry is almost completely created due to various incentive structures or overt benefits provided by the state. Capitalism results in an efficient organization of industry, however, this is even to the detriment of morality as it relates to higher principles. The problem

---

[4] Mostly of the private variety.

[5] The jewish question is not the topic of the book and will not be discussed any further.

with banks is that the state makes efficient banking synonymous with exploitative business practices. This has resulted in banks having deteriorated from their proper position in society and becoming entities that are not needed nor wanted. We can criticize capitalism for not functioning inefficiently in spite of incentives, but if capitalism functioned inefficiently, then capitalism would be a useless system in itself. The systematic exploitation exhibited by the modern banking system is due to the state.

Capitalism as an economic system can not be blamed for the follies of the state and as such, it would become an irrelevant question when talking about capitalism. But for the state to even matter it is necessary to first demonstrate that banking by itself is not exploitative. Capitalists and bankers can co-operate with the state, but any results of state policy reflect on the state and not on capitalism, we ought to look at what pure capitalism has to provide in such conflicts. It is important to clarify here that I am only talking about capitalism as an economic system and not in a political or a philosophical context.

Banking serves two large functions, first is the storage of money in order to reduce transaction costs and protect monetary reserves. When money is stored within a system where it is accessible from multiple locations and which can be easily managed from ledgers, transacting money is much easier than it otherwise would be. Essentially to rearrange the property rights in any financial dealings, you only need two co-operative banks to rearrange their financial records to demonstrate that the transaction has taken place. This results in the bank giving the property right to the fixed quantity of money to the person the money was transferred to. This mitigates any need for interpersonal exchanges of commodities and in an economy that uses digital technology, banks can also abolish the need for banknotes when inconvenient. People no longer need to carry around even a physical representation of currency and can function solely using the systems in place to allow for transactions to take place. This is due to the invention of the credit card and the debit card. In this manner, banks benefit everyone.

Banking also provides increased security that an individual would not otherwise have, this is because banks can store currency or commodities in safe locations where they are not under threat. This is effective in reducing crime and also increases efficiency in the economy insofar as crime is prevented. People do not need to lack confidence in the monetary reserves they have as they can only be physically stolen if the bank is overpowered. Due to the ability to concentrate resources in banks, there is no need to assume that banks are easily overpowered. And even if banks are overpowered, they still can use their resources to recuperate their losses better than any individual could. When it comes to the storage of currency, it is hard to say that they are ever in safer places than banks from the perspective of pure raw might. Banks are some of the most secure locations for very good reasons.

The second function of banks is the reallocation of resources to purposes in which they are in better use than they were before. If someone has a large amount of funds without use, they can utilize the bank to earn additional money on their first principal investment, this is done through lending and investment. However, there can be an objection that lending money in itself is exploitative and the same argument for investment. The point of this argument is that by investing and lending one is able to make money without contributing anything. Whether it is the labour of the person trying to pay back the money or the labour of the people who run the companies which pay dividends, the person who lends money will get more money without labouring. However, the very important thing to note here is that money denotes resources. This may be lost in accounting fiction, but ultimately money is a store of value and value is obtained from physical goods and services.

Since value is obtained from physical goods and services and since money can be exchanged for these goods and services, the person lending or investing is essentially selling goods and services with the ability to pay back later instead of now. The money he then earns is the premium for being paid back later instead of the very moment he provides these goods and services for the person he invests into or lends to. This premium is solely due to it being an inconvenience to have to wait for payment, it compensates for the risk taken and the time spent waiting. Without politically charged rhetoric, it seems like the banking system is quite innocuous, it reduces transaction costs, increases security and allocates resources more efficiently than they were allocated before, thus there are only two more objections to the pure form of banking.

First, there is the objection that everyone should have access to resources and that the need to allocate them through banks and with interest is in itself inhumane. But this is inconceivable, there is no superabundance of all resources. This means that really the available options are that either resources are allocated privately or they are allocated publicly. Either people contribute from their own personal wealth or some collective fund managed by councils or bureaucracies which uses the wealth of those forced to pay them. Why is the second option more inherently appealing than the first one is? If we assume that people only serve the common good or their own selfish interest, then it's only a small leap to favour public management of property over private. Private management of wealth may bring the middle class and the rich products that are fun or entertaining in a selfish way, but public management will obviously result in vital public projects for the poor, such as water and housing for everyone.

But here we must ignore that unless resources are managed directly and democratically, as the socialist anarchists wish them to be, the persons in charge of managing the resources will still look out for their own selfish interests. If people are allowed to use resources on their own, they will spend them in areas that they gain from. This means that everyone who has any value to offer can spend money as he wishes on things that benefit him. If officials manage resources they will use their control over the resources to increase their power with no cost to themselves as they are not the ones paying for the resources. Councils and bureaus only have the ability to delegate where these resources are being utilized. It will become inevitable that resources will only be eventually used for the good of the people who do the allocating of the resources. And this is not even considering "bread and circuses[6]", the public functionaries will secure their power by giving the masses back what they took from the masses.

The same is true in capitalism, however, there is an innate ability to allocate resources for yourself by selling your labour or your products. This is true no matter how many resources other people have. They may be in stronger market positions, but that does not prevent you from using your innate abilities in ways that you think will be useful. Banking helps facilitate this method of exchange. Some sects of more liberal socialistic thought are against banks because they too will inevitably allocate resources to their own profit, but this is irrelevant as the banks only profit as long as everyone else profits. In a pure capitalist system, if the bank fails to allocate resources efficiently, it will not earn any money. There is no bailout without the state deciding to save the failing banks. This is because the bank generates no income on its own and needs to use the resources it has access to create income and a portion of this income will go to the people who the bank functionally lent money from.

In essence, when explained simply, banking is innocuous at worst. This does not mean that every bank is innocuous, but there is nothing inherently corrupt or wrong about banks, at least if we discount the objections raised by fascist or religious theory. The only way banks are inherently malignant is if we completely oppose money on principle. This too is a valid concern and it is

---

[6] The modern equivalent of which being welfare and football stadiums.

understandable why socialists would direct their focus on money. In a capitalistic economy, they say, money attracts a special value that would not be there in other forms of economic organization. People start to desire money not because they want to buy something, but rather simply because they want money for the sake of money as money provides status and perceived value. Due to this, they find it preferable to form a pseudo-economy without any monetary transactions and as such, they oppose banks due to them being the main sources of money.

And in a socialistic economy, the pseudo-equality will ensure that the amount of money each person has would become less relevant no matter what the specifics are. So it is also possible to organize the distribution of resources without any money involved. If resources are then distributed completely democratically, as the anarchists describe, then you would also avoid the problem of individual power and it would result in a social order in which you can oppose banks. And for obvious reasons this is enticing. A society in which each person is required to contribute to the society, but in return will be taken care of by the society is a concept many are drawn towards. However, the problem with this sort of society is twofold. First, there are no centralized institutions and it becomes hard to undertake large projects. This can be solved but is still a valid concern. The second issue is the inevitable downward distribution that will take place with the most valuable economic positions.

It is inevitable that if every position is open, people will choose the positions that are the most valued socially, that is how much personal benefit people can gain from working those jobs. There is only a limited amount of incentive to work harder and take more responsibility when there is no money or private property. This means that what will eventually happen is that the most valuable members of society will drop out of the workforce as much as they possibly can and focus on their personal endeavours. Less valuable members will eventually do the work of the most valuable in part and the quality of these positions will lessen making them inherently less valuable. If the positions are less valuable, the originally qualified workers may entirely drop out of the position leaving only the unqualified within these positions[7].

This is a condition that everyone should want to avoid and which is impossible to avoid under a socialistic and anarchistic system. No matter what steps socialists take to argue against banking purely on principle, they will eventually end up at some form of roadblock and reach an undesirable system from the perspective of any sort of social organization. It is still possible to prefer systems that are greatly inefficient, but this preference can only stem from decisively valuing equality over wealth. What socialists could do instead is reorganize banking to be owned by the workers, even upon doing this socialists can still logically be socialists. If a socialist wishes to be rational in their critique of capitalism, they should want to seize the means of banking and not

---

[7]

This is true at least as long as there is no fundamental equality within humans. However, both intellectual and physical ability is largely influenced by genetics, thus there is no way in which we can assume that there is fundamental equality. Even if there is perfect biological equality, if free will exists, there will be tremendous sociological inequality.

abolish banks[8]. But there are still important problems as they relate to the way banks are run right now.

When the socialists point to the power structures in society as they relate to banks and the perpetual servitude of the population to various banking institutions, they are not wrong. This is empirically and historically is the result of government and not of capitalism. Thus it would be useful to just ignore that capitalism is involved in the equation, but doing that would be misguided. Libertarians have a bad tendency to call statist capitalism either corporatism or straight up fascism, this makes no sense when we consider the historical conditions of capitalism. We must accept that not all capitalism is pure and can create power structures when enmeshed with the state. The banks are a great store of wealth and thus they will obviously have a great influence over a state[9]. The state will thrive off rich benefactors and will create legislation that favours the capitalists. All the exploitation and immoral practices we see with banks can be traced back to some sort of state incentive. It's not that banks are inherently the most profitable as giant scams, but when the government is controlled by the banks, the banks will strive to make uselessness and unwise inaction the most profitable paths that they can take.

8

    The reasons for why this is suboptimal are described in the previous chapter.

9

    At least this is true provided that the class character of the state is fundamentally capitalist, a perfect socialist state would only be responsible for leading the revolution. There has been no historical evidence of this happening. Whenever socialism has been tried, it has always resulted in socialism collapsing into an impure system before it could deliver a utopia.

And since banks, by necessity, hold onto a great deal of wealth, the state will be controlled by banks. All finances in a modern economy have to go through the bank due to how much influence the banks have had over the accepted structure of legislation. Thus the banks are functionally in control over all the resources in society and this is demonstrated by legislation around the world ensuring that banks have temporary ownership of all their wares. This should be unacceptable to any capitalist and socialist. The control over society by banks, as enabled by the state, should not be something characteristic of any political system. However, it is inevitable that when there is no abolition of the state or a complete separation of the state and economy, in a capitalist system, the banks will control the society.

However, since this is only possible due to the state we must criticize the state for redistributing property rights in a manner that benefits the banks over the consumers of the banks and the workers in society. This is an argument against the state even if you would like to frame it as an argument against the capitalistic economic and social system. Without a redistribution of property rights, the proprietors of the funds in banks would be the people who deposited those funds and not the banks themselves. Due to this banks could never become such behemoth organizations with near-total complete control over the economy as they would actually be responsible to someone else.

We can conclude that banking is an inherently dangerous industry whenever we have a state and that there can be no peaceful coexistence of banking and the state without creating an economic system dominated by banks. However, this should not serve as a condemnation of banking itself, but rather of the state having influence over the capitalist economy. The market tends to profit those who act according to the incentives provided and if the incentives provided allow for parasitism the market will provide parasites. However, banking is quite innocuous on its own without access to state violence and not a threat unless it is allowed to become one. The inner machinations of banks are not necessarily repressive or exploitative, but rather serve to increase social wealth and comfort. Only in systems where there is artificial overcomplication through the state or other means can banks become more than agents of money management and start to take a commanding role in the economy. We can criticize banking as it is right now without completely conceding that capitalism as a system will always be exploitative.

V – Exploitation

Supposedly under the system of capitalism. there is a great amount of exploitation when it comes to the working class, the workers in this society are assumed to be treated unfairly and thus there is an innate problem with capitalism. This problem stems from the conflict between the classes of the workers and the capitalists being in a relationship where the capitalists are the exploiters. Simply put, the capitalist is any person who sells access to his capital on the market and a worker is any person who buys access to this capital, or in other words, sells his labour. The act of buying capital produces so-called surplus value for the capitalist when he is able to sell access to capital while not losing his right to the capital. The cost of buying capital for the worker is then simply the exploitation inherent within the capitalist system as the capitalist class has the capital they can sell and the working class needs to buy capital.

Since these are the buyers and sellers on the market, they have contradictory incentives which will meet at an economic equilibrium at some point. Those who sell access to capital, or in other words the capitalists, want to raise the price of capital as high as possible, to do this they have to either increase the value of capital or the demand for capital in one way or another. The workers want to raise the price of labour as they buy access to capital by using their labour, to do this they have to either increase the value of labour or the demand for labour. Both sides can also increase the price of either capital or labour by contracting the supply of the other class. In essence, the price of labour goes up when there is less capital and the price of capital goes up when there is less labour. There are more parts to this class analysis and they are also important, but this fundamental economic conflict is supposedly contradictory to and unsustainable as there is a constant drive to contract capital and to make capital more expensive which will drive capitalism as a system to self-destruct.

The traditional terms used by both capitalists and socialists do not put this into the terms of buying and selling capital in exchange for labour or labour in exchange for capital. In most economics, it is thought that those selling capital are always buying labour as we can see a monetary transaction on the market where the capitalists give workers money while workers produce goods. Thus in most texts, you can see those terms used that signify this approach to the labour market, but that is fundamentally misguided. A capitalist can buy capital and land only because he has property rights to that capital and that land. If the capitalist is not functioning within a system of indentured servitude, it is impossible to buy property rights in labour. The worker is also an acting man in the economy and as much of a buyer as the capitalist is, the exchange between the capitalist and the labourer is fundamentally an exchange of capital and labour, not money and labour or money and capital. The money wages earned by the worker are the result of the capitalist buying the goods the worker produced, the money surplus earned by the capitalist is the result of the worker purchasing access to the capital that the capitalist has.

However, this assumes that the capitalist class is by necessity a ruling class and if we use the marxist definition of capitalism this may be the case. But marxist definitions are not the arbiters of all language. Most people understand capitalism as the private ownership of the means of production, or more accurately the decentralized management of mundane operations and the private collection of profits. If we use this definition there are three possible outcomes, the capitalists are the ruling class, the workers are the ruling class or there are no ruling classes. When the capitalists are the ruling class there will be an increase in the price of capital and it will be perpetual and as great as it can be[10]. This results in the exploitation of the worker as the worker is subject to institutional increases in the price of capital. These institutional increases in the price of capital are accurately understood as exploitation.

Because this is the case and because the price of capital is increased institutionally, the equilibrium between labour and capital cannot be met, this means that there will be some perpetual underemployment of the people who simply cannot afford the price of capital at the increased cost. Without this barrier, net-productive people would always find employment, provided the economy has time to adjust in the case of abrupt changes. Furthermore, with the price of capital being inflated, there is more competition between the people who strive to acquire access to

---

[10] An interesting insight produced by this approach that the problem of infinite expansion in a finite system mainly refers to the fact that capitalists will eventually be unable to raise the price of capital. This cannot condemn the entire free market economy.

renting capital. This creates a scenario where the workers raise the prices of capital even further by competing with one another. By raising the price of capital the capitalists also inherently increase the demand for capital as fewer people can get access to capital. Thus they contract the supply of labour and create a scenario where the working class is perpetually at the whims of the capitalists. This can be accomplished in multiple direct or indirect ways, most require access to state power.

First, the capitalist can attempt to raise prices without a general increase in wages in the economy, this would allow the capitalist to create a greater necessity for more capital and a greater competition for capital. Second, the capitalist can get the state to institute prohibitions for work, which indirectly reduce the value of labour by raising the general level of wages without such an increase in the productive powers in the people working. This can be done through income taxation, regulation and minimum wage laws as they result in workers earning less through no fault of their own and thus creating an artificial scarcity of capital. Income taxes directly take from the worker and minimum wages create new submarginal workers who are now unable to get jobs. Regulation adds to the cost of hiring workers without creating additional benefits for the capitalist. So thus we can say that protections for the consumer and the worker actually often benefit the capitalist when we look at general economic power.

Consumers may have higher quality goods and workers may have higher quality workplaces, but there will be fewer goods and less accessible capital in the economy with the same amount of labourers. Further increasing the competition for capital and creating an even larger degree of increase in the price when it comes to gaining access to capital. The workers need to expend more labour to get access to a lesser amount of capital as the capitalists do not need to compete with one another due to the artificial scarcity of capital.

This partly also hinges on the ability for the capitalist to restrict the entry of new capital into the system. There cannot be an increased supply of capital to offset the increased price. This is usually created by using the government to inflate costs or outright prohibit people from doing business. By doing this, the capitalists can restrict the amount of capital and the economic productivity of capital thus creating a larger demand for the scarce capital that exists. We would expect to see a system like we see right now where wages are stagnant while the capitalist class gets wealthier. This is not to say that the stagnation of wages is only the doing of capitalists. Many pro-labour efforts and other statist programs have also contributed to the same effect as their legislation mistakenly aids the capitalist class. There are also other effects which may contribute to the stagnation of wages.

The opposite possibility to the domination of capital is the economy where workers are in power and are the ruling class. Some would contend that this would logically imply the destruction of the capitalists and the capitalist system, but we can imagine a world where the workers, upon achieving their class domination, determine that it is beneficial to keep the system of capital. Here the workers would aim to reduce the cost of gaining access to capital or increase the value of labour within the capitalist system. This would result in people obtaining access to capital below the point of market equilibrium and thus there would be an overconsumption of capital. This means that capital will be utilized by too many people in such a manner that eventually there will either be a collapse of the capitalist system or a stable increase in poverty as capital runs out. When workers can use the capital they want below the cost that the market would set with the profit rates of the capitalist greatly reduced, there would be a generalized wealth redistribution from the capitalist class to the working class.

However, this would also mean that the entire system of capital would become unsustainable as there is no longer enough capital to operate the complex chains of production. At least in the manner in which they did before, the excess of people working on the limited capital will always use more capital than otherwise would have been used. If the workers were the ruling class, we would see at least a great collapse in capitalism as the capital eventually runs out and is unable to produce at the previous levels when there is too much labour in comparison to the amount of capital. In this manner, there would also have to be such a drastic reorganization of the economy that it would not even resemble the capitalist system of production and thus create a system more akin to socialism.

It is also conceivable that the workers might try to get the capitalists to increase the amount of capital in the economy to make it less scarce while preserving the value of the labour. This is unlikely as it is less possible to coerce the capitalists to produce capital that will be useless to themselves as it is to allow access to workers who will overconsume the capital without providing the capitalist the profits necessary to maintain that capital. However, if the workers could somehow overproduce capital so that the capital was commonly available and abundant and thus almost worthless, they would create a system in which full worker democracy would be established. This is because the capitalists no longer can assert any of their demands and will have to do their best to retain even meager profits. The capitalists would completely be relegated to the role of entrepreneur and manager with no additional gain from these tasks. This may be favoured by many, but the manager and the entrepreneur perform tasks which depend entirely on the compensation being worth the task. We would eventually see an end to the entrepreneurs and the managers. This also leads to socialism, which is desirable for the socialist and truly the inevitable result of the workers controlling the capitalist system.

It seems inevitable that either the capitalist class will retain control over the economy until it is no longer sustainable or the working class will rise up and rule over the economy, turning it into socialism. Thus, accepting these premises it may seem as if socialism is truly inevitable and the natural end of economic history. When the capitalist class controls the economy they can exploit workers via institutionally raising the prices of capital and in such a manner there is worker exploitation. When the working class controls the economy, the economy would have to be so drastically restructured that it could not even resemble a capitalist economy. Thus it is simple for many to conclude that the only choices we have are between worker exploitation and socialism, if we are not capitalists, we should always side with socialism as otherwise. we would be dooming ourselves to be exploited by those who do own capital.

However there is another solution[11], that solution is that no class has ruling power over the economy. When this is the case, there can be no worker exploitation and there can be no collapse of capitalism as the equilibrium in the price needed for access to capital is constantly upheld. This means that there are no excess profits but rather the rightly earned profits as decided through the market and there is also no overconsumption of capital as there is the barrier to the capital that excludes the destructive labourers. By having no class rule there is a system where there is functionally no actual worker exploitation and which can still be described as a capitalist economy. But this is impossible or near-impossible as long as the state exists, this is because the state will always be subject to some pressure group or other and thus will always either create a system dominated by the capitalists or dominated by the workers.

We can't simply assert, as many conservatives and libertarians do, that there are no class distinctions inherent in capitalism and

---

[11]

If we would want to get extremely specific there is also the corporatist or syndicalist way, we can imagine a system where both capitalists and workers rule and retain a degree of control over the economy. This is the premise of some forms of national or guild syndicalism and the fascism that eventually developed out of it; the control of the economy by all classes through the government. Al classes could achieve their goals through the state without any class dominating, this may be inefficient in the abstract but by legislating the other class or forming agreements through the state, it provides a "third position".

thus there is no need to avoid the rule of a certain class. Asserting this is naive at best. We also cannot simply say that the state should have nothing to do with the economy, as by existing the state already has control over the economy. The state creates legislative law, collects revenue and presumably controls some degree of industry. The only solution to the problem of worker exploitation, which is not socialism, becomes having capitalism without a state. Capitalism where there is no legitimized user of force and no legitimate legislator of law. When this is the case, there can be no entity that can contract the supply of labour to increase the demand for capital or raise the price for capital. There can also be no artificial costs to entry which allow capitalists to retain their monopolies, which would make control over the workers impossible even if capitalists tried to cartelize and control the economy.

The argument could then be made that whenever there are protections to private property, the capitalists are inherently the ruling class as the capitalists own the majority of the property. But as established before worker exploitation can only be defined as the unwarranted costs of acquiring access to capital. If it is exploitative to be excluded from the market for capital by force if the worker is unwilling to pay for the access, then it must also be exploitative to withhold any resource from anyone else. In this manner, the socialists must either admit a breakdown in their dichotomy of private and personal property[12] or admit that capitalism is not inherently exploitative. Socialists can either

---
12

accept that it is not unjust to restrict the access to capital, but that it is also unjust to restrict the access to toothbrushes when someone is in need of a toothbrush and someone else has a toothbrush. Capitalism can still be criticized in a plethora of ways, but it cannot be described as inherently exploitative, provided that the simple act of exclusion is not exploitation. If the simple act of exclusion is inherently exploitation, then all acts of exclusion are.

Here, there can be one more argument that the exclusion from capital fundamentally dooms a person to starvation and a life of guaranteed misery and an early death, but a socialist state or commune would not be able to provide everything to everyone either. No reasonable socialist favours the access to all goods by all people if these people do not contribute anything to society and are able to work. The socialists could accept the caricature of just wanting to give people free stuff and ignore the centuries of theory that they have themselves accumulated, but by doing so they concede that socialism does enable laziness and that the arguments against socialism from that perspective are correct.

However, if the costs to access capital are raised artificially there can form an exploitative capitalism, in this case, people are institutionally excluded from access to capital and not personally excluded from access to capital. Thus there would be a true surplus value and a true domination of the capitalist class which would be directly parasitic in regards to the working class. As long as the

---

A large tool in socialist rhetoric is claiming that depending on occupancy and use, there is a fundamental distinction between personal and private property. This mostly boils down to the notion that all property that is not rented is not really private property.

price of access to capital is at the point of equilibrium, there is in no meaningful sense an exploitation of one class or another, but rather the simple laws of supply and demand allocating resources in an efficient manner.

As an aside, there are also the concerns that workers will fundamentally be alienated from themselves, their labour and one another due to the way the capitalist system works, this is most often related to worker exploitation but it deserves a separate mention. Supposedly workers are alienated from themselves because they do not control what they do. Workers are also alienated from their labour because they do not control what is done with what they produce. And workers are also alienated from one another since relations become ones of capital as workers themselves become alienated from themselves. This plays into the human experience that finds work as an unpleasant task and can easily provide an answer for why it is that people do not enjoy work. But this assumes that work is something that should be enjoyed and not simply just a necessity for human survival.

Workers may not be in control of themselves when they work for a capitalist, but they will never be in control of themselves when there is work. No matter if the worker works for a collective or on a farm, he is still subject to what his work demands of him. Having a different structure of work will only result in the worker being alienated in a different way. The only answer to this is to be completely anti-work, which falls upon a whole set of different problems by itself. No matter what the work is and whether production is for use or exchange, the worker will be alienated from his labour as his labour will by necessity be used by someone else for some other purpose as otherwise, the work would have been completely meaningless. This is unless the worker wants to enjoy the tremendous benefits of autarky, such as starvation and early death from illness.

The notion that in capitalism relationships between different persons become solely ones of capital is fundamentally absurd as capital has no life in itself but rather is representative of the organization of the economy. The way people relate to one another is independent of the economy insofar as they relate to each other in a way that does not translate to the wider economy. Asserting that relations between individuals in capitalism are simply relations of capital is misguided as it assumes that people have no interests outside of capital. As long as people themselves do not give up their personality in order to become mindless automatons, there is no possibility of anyone reducing their own life to capital. It is a possibility that people within capital do surrender themselves to capital, but this is a phenomenon which has other social causes and is not inherent in every capitalist system.

VI – Capital Accumulation[13]

A central argument by socialists against the entire system of capitalism is that of capital accumulation, this usually takes one of three forms. Personal capital accumulation, capital accumulation by corporations and intergenerational capital accumulation. Socialists think that all of these phenomena are bad things since they reinforce different systems of dominance on the market and destroy all semblance of fair competition. In more common terms what socialists oppose is saving, successful enterprise and inheritance. This may seem like a rational set of problems to oppose for socialists, but when deconstructed is instead one of the most ridiculous attempts at attempting to showcase socialism as not a strictly egalitarian project but also one that can trump capitalism in meritocracy by giving everyone an equal chance. For reasons discussed below this is ludicrous.

First, there is the notion that savings and further investing somehow inherently gives an unfair advantage to the person who saved his money as he is able to make money from money and not from his labour. Thus, the socialists want to eliminate this ability and not let people charge interest or to invest money to prohibit any income that is supposedly unearned. However, saying that saving is simply gaining money out of thin air misses the point completely. To save money one needs to consume less when one

---

[13] Due to the way the chapters were not written chronologically, there is a significant amount of overlap between this chapter and the one on investing. It is safe to skim or skip the first part of the chapter. It is still original content with some new insights, however, the general themes are very similar.

consumes less they can save money and profit from the money they save. If one wants to maintain their consumption habits and not save, it is they who put themselves at an institutional disadvantage. A socialist can then contend that the problem is not fact that people save, but rather that only the upper class is able to save while the lower classes have to spend all their money to survive, thus cutting off an income stream from the workers while the capitalists rapidly increase the degree of capital that they have in society.

But this too makes no sense, even the poorest in society spend money on things that are not strictly necessary. Nothing material excludes poor people from saving money, but rather the lack of their ability to earn more money than they want to use for consumption. If the poor wanted to consume less or if they earned more money and kept the consumption at the same level, they could reach the same sort of capital accumulation that the upper class has. However, being unable to do this is only a personal folly and not something that is strictly institutional. The poorest in modern society can afford to live at standards previously unheard of in most places around the world. In the West and in Asia, this means a rapid increase in the quality of living. In the rest of the world additional wealth means a rapid increase in reproductive rates. The poorest have the luxury of living at higher standards than kings used to or reproducing at rates previously unheard of.

And finally, there is the theoretical concern of a rich person being able to delegate all their duties to someone else and just coasting off the capital they have without putting any effort into that capital. This fundamentally would defeat the capitalist notion that the rich know what to do with their money and contribute to society and would lend further credence to the notion that the capitalists are only parasitical entities upon society. This theoretical possibility to live off of rents and investments is viewed as a negative, but why is it so? Simply restricting the access to capital and ensuring that it is allocated to proper purposes is enough of a social role for a person who has this amount of money. They are unable to make any great profits when they delegate all decision making to other parties, but if the rich are fine with simply a moderately comfortable life, then there should be no problem with them not doing anything with their capital other than delegating its use. But more profits that can be earned with entrepreneurship and personal involvement in business management. This is why most rich people actually retain control over their capital and do not delegate it to other people so as to live a decently comfortable life.

This also means that any rich person is liable to lose all their money and break their own hegemony. And this is not all, there is a natural process of attrition in the upper classes when we don't assume perfect prudence. Increased consumption with increased money leads to a more decadent lifestyle, but it assumes that the wealth remains. When the rich are not able to cut the extravagances in their lifestyle when they prove to have invested into unsustainable businesses, the capital will gradually shift to the remainder of the society in the form of other people investing and the rich buying consumer goods. Since most people find it hard to stop spending their money, money ends up back in the economy in one way or another. If any person, wealthy or not, can't maintain their income they will lose their wealth.

The best argument when it comes to capital accumulation is the problem of capital accumulation by certain companies. When corporations are successful they make more money and when they make more money, they can invest further into themselves and theoretically, this should allow for the market to be dominated by a select few businesses. Except in reality we are faced with the problem where this does not actually happen. Companies rise and fall not based on the amount of total wealth they can amass, but rather based on the efficiency with which they operate and the novelty of what they can bring to the market. The sort of free market monopolization is always temporary due to the inefficient nature of large businesses. The supposed capital accumulation does not actually manage to sustain these oligarchies. Furthermore, owning capital inherently prevents innovation as capital can't be easily repurposed for other uses. This means that the larger a company is, the harder it is for that company to adapt to changing market conditions and the more likely it is to fail if the management errs.

There has been no case in history where a certain company kept a stable monopoly over an industry without the help of the government, no matter how much that company may have held the share of the market at any point, competitive pressures have always brought them down. Furthermore, even theoretically this does not make sense, companies can spend money on themselves to a supposedly boundless extent, but if they are already so successful as to amass a significant amount of money, it is to be expected that they are already nearing the most efficient size of their firm. Every firm has an optimal size in which they can create an economy of scale, but also not get bogged down in administrative problems. Corporations above or below this size are less competitive than other corporations. Thus we can expect that businesses that are as profitable as to gain these immense amounts of wealth are also businesses that are near their optimal size. Increasing the size of corporate structures is not a solution to everything and this logic does not seem to hold up.

And finally, there is the intergenerational capital accumulation which happens through following generations gaining access to the capital of their parents. This results in a scenario where supposedly there are hegemonic families and there is no social mobility or opportunity for the children of poor families, this is further reinforced by education and the lack of connections. This perceivedly gives an unfair upper hand to the children of rich families and perpetuates the unmeritocratic nature of capitalism by allowing these children to keep the money they only gained access to unearnedly. Thus to combat this we need to at the bare minimum eliminate inheritance so intergenerational capital accumulation could not take place. But this issue is one ultimately of perspective and not of morality.

It is not the child that ought to be the focal point, but rather the parents, when inheritance is eliminated you will simply see less work being done as the ultimate reward of being able to give your child an easier life is impossible to achieve. Or it may result in worse spending habits as people have no need to take care of their potential children to the extent that they previously would have done due to the legal restrictions on inheritance. The parents possess all the resources while the child has none. Because parents have control over these resources and the children lack any resources at all the fundamental social analysis should not be directed towards the children but rather the parents.

We can still trace sociological capital accumulation trends in families and find that a lot of people who inherit a lot of money fail to live up to their parents and lose most of the wealth without recuperating it. Thus it is not a manner of eternal hegemony but rather the similar sort of attrition as discussed earlier. The market is not a rapid actor but the adjustments in the market will take place according to the degree of the imperfection on behalf of the rich inheritors. Eventually, if these children turn out to be unworthy, then they will lose their money as has been demonstrated by countless accounts in which this exact scenario has happened. Thus it cannot be said that capitalism, by necessity, creates any intergenerational class structure due to perpetual capital accumulation.

And finally there is the question of education, which should not be a question at all. This is because everyone who has extremely high levels of intelligence is usually able to get an education. However, as intelligence is heritable to a degree we must recognize that less intelligent parents produce less intelligent children and that poorer people tend to be less intelligent, this is just due to the tendency of intelligent people not to stay poor. There is still enough variance and deviation that if poor people got a better education, they would be better situated in the economy. However, this ignores that the roles in any economy, socialist or capitalist, are very varied and there are requirements for manual labour and for intellectual labour. There are people for whom education is a strictly negative endeavour as they are never going to be able to utilize their education and only experience the opportunity cost of using their time for education while they could have been doing something else.

This may be an imperfect and undesirable state of affairs and if everything was perfect, each person would gain intellectual fulfilment from their labour. But until we are able to automate all manual jobs, educating everyone is simply cruelty and leads to them not being able to get work that corresponds to their level of education. The tendency for modern society to unjustly condemn manual labour only aggravates this and does not let the economy sort itself out. We should respect the dignity of the manual labourer and not imply that intellectual labour is the only thing worthwhile.

Anarchist Critiques

I – Freedom

Anarchists often say that there is no true freedom when workers are subject to the whims of their bosses since the workers are not completely independent so long as they have to rely on capitalists. They can't determine their own direction in life as they need to do what they are told to do by the capitalist class and as such capitalism is incompatible with true freedom. Since the workers aren't truly free, it doesn't matter how much we preach choice and free markets as that only means that we want choices and markets for the bosses and not for the lower classes. And since people without land or capital can either work for a capitalist or die from starvation, the labourers must rely on the capitalists and they can never experience freedom whenever there is a capitalist system.

No matter what liberty we may offer in theory, it only means that we want liberty for the capitalists. The only way the workers can get liberated is by egalitarian capital structures without the state, which capitalism does not allow for as the workers still need to participate in hierarchical systems. The ownership of capital and land is a hierarchical system, only a limited amount of people can own private property on which others have to work. Until private property is completely abolished, there can be no question about whether or not the workers are free. Even if capitalism made workers more prosperous, it also removed liberty.

Furthermore, these people argue that no one can reasonably remove themselves from the capitalist system, there is no way to be completely anarchistic when there is any influence by the capitalists as they will do anything to shut down any anarchist movement. This means that there will necessarily be some amount of violent repression when any anarchist experiment is formed since the capitalists do not want to lose their hegemony. There will always be a need for force and violence as when anarchists could establish their own way of life and offer an alternative to the working class, capitalists would become completely defunct. Thus, the class interest of the capitalists is always fundamentally threatened by anarchists and the capitalists will always fight back against anarchists. The only way to be free is then via a complete abolition of the capitalist system. The anarchists need to get rid of capitalism before the working class can be liberated from all authority.

The first thing we have to establish is that libertarians must share the goal with anarchists to gain the right to establish anarchistic collectives. This means that even though we may disagree with socialistic forms of organization which are integral to anarchism, we must agree with the right for anarchists to organize as long as they are not disruptive towards other people. Even though we are supporters of capitalism, we must also support the right for each person to self-determine and decide to not be involved in the capitalist system. We must, therefore, oppose capitalist intrusions into anarchistic experiments as long as they are unwarranted.

But this does not mean that we need to ensure the right for anarchists to seize the means of production or to topple the capitalist system in a violent revolution. If anarchists cannot peaceably demonstrate the advantages of their system, they do not deserve to have a platform on which they can establish their society. If anarchists can really contend with the capitalist mode of production to such an extent that the capitalists must infringe on them to stop the complete collapse of capitalism, anarchists will not need to seize any means of production. If the alternative is desirable enough, it would result in anarchists getting resources from capitalists peacefully in due time. Anarchists may not morally care about any property rights, but practically we should defend anarchists against any intrusions upon their property[14] and defend ourselves against any intrusions by the anarchists. But this also means that eventually, property rights may go defunct as all workers decide to go on a generalized strike or simply stop recognizing property. In that way, the anarchists can get control over the means of production and thus peacefully abolish capitalism. Socialist economic principles or worker-run co-operatives could also outcompete the capitalist system, thus getting rid of capitalism. This would be as capitalism could not theoretically stand against these systems, at least from the anarchist framework. However, if this stateless form of socialism cannot offer enough value to the working classes, it will simply die out by its own hand.

These are all peaceful ways to achieve an anarchist society once we have first achieved a libertarian society and none of them require any violence. We must also support anarchists if they can

---

[14] This does not imply physical defence where lives are risked, but rather defence in the sense of discussion and practical philosophy.

demonstrate the advantages of socialistic organization in a free manner. Anarchists should have the freedom to separate from capitalism if workers are really oppressed, but they are not entitled to anything more. If anarchists cannot demonstrate how their system is better, then it is a problem with socialism and not that they are suppressed by capitalists and not that the capitalists do not allow for them to gain access to the means of production. In anarchist theory, workers produce all value, which means that workers should be able to produce this value even without access to the capital that was saved in the past by the capitalists restricting their consumption. The anarchists do not need capitalists and can function off of natural resources and the means that they previously acquired. Furthermore, these workers can still try to obtain funding and resources in a decentralized manner from other workers who want to see an anarchist society established without themselves founding such a society.

Thus if libertarian capitalists can achieve their goal, the anarchists are provided with multiple ways to achieve what they want to ultimately achieve. This means that the people who promote pure untainted capitalism do not try to disallow any kind of freedom and the anarchists should at least be on board with this movement. In opportunist terms, libertarianism guarantees that anarchists themselves would be able to establish their own societies. Furthermore, these are only just the ways in which one can achieve socialistic freedom within a libertarian system when one assumes that there is no freedom to be found in a libertarian system. Not only does capitalism in the purest, libertarian sense allow for the greatest chance to establish anarchism, I would contend that freedom within anarchism is much overestimated when compared with libertarian freedom.

Libertarians are less oriented on freedom than anarchists, this is certain as libertarians have property as their primary principle instead of freedom for the sake of freedom. The freedom described by the libertarians is the freedom to own yourself and your own property without any interference from other parties. This conflicts with notions of absolute freedom as any person is only free as long as they do not infringe on the property of any other person or do not break contracts they have formed previously. The only restrictions to freedom in a libertarian society are the restrictions that are created by having the right to own property. Thus the question becomes whether owning property is more important to freedom than being able to do what you want to do with the property of other people. If it is true that the right to own property is vital to freedom then it is true that the right to own property creates more freedom than it takes away. This may be counterintuitive to anarchists as property is a restriction upon some freedoms. But we also must understand that any freedom has in itself the ability to take away other people's freedom, there is no freedom that has no innate ability to rob others of their freedom.

If property is integral to maintaining a free society, it is no longer true that workers are forced to work for capitalists, but rather that workers themselves do not have the capital needed to live in abundance by themselves and if they want a high quality of life need to work for a capitalist. When that is the case it's also true that the workers as a class are not oppressed by capitalists as the working class and capitalist class are bound by contractual relations and not hegemonic bonds. A worker is simply a person who has not yet had the chance to accumulate capital, the hierarchy is completely established by all the people involved in the hierarchy and not by oppression or compulsion. Free markets will truly be free for everyone and liberty will be liberty for everyone, however, we run into one more problem while trying to tackle this question.

There are multiple interpretations of freedom based on moral systems, we cannot always just say that freedom is the increased ability to do what you want. In this case, we could take the definition of freedom to be the ability to make the widest array of choices with desirable results. That is that each person can best choose what to do with their lives in productive manners. This is still somewhat moralistic but it is still a reasonable assumption and it is not a given that one side must win from this assumption. There can be both an argument that anarchism results in maximum freedom as managers and capitalists cannot suck up resources from the economy, which in turn allows for better control by the working class over their own lives. Or it could be that libertarianism results in maximum freedom as people are allowed to own property and thus make the best decisions and gain the benefits of their decisions.

If we take freedom as simply the least amount of institutional restrictions, then we would have to conclude that anarchism can provide for the highest degree of freedom. This means simply that more things are allowed under anarchism than under libertarianism. However, the fact that more things are allowed does not necessarily mean anything in reality as anarchism must disallow all exclusive claims to property. This means that even though fewer prohibitions are present in anarchism, there are still prohibitions against forming prohibitions. This results in an inevitable contradiction as is the case with any model of freedom that sees freedom as simply the highest array of choices, even though it may not be the optimal definition, we should view freedom as being the ability to do what you want with your time and your labour and get the most out of it.

Under an anarchist system, there are no systems of hierarchy and as such the workers get the full benefits of their labour without the state or the capitalist class appropriating any of the work that has been done by the workers for their own gain. Broadly put, this means that the workers have control over the means of production and any profit that previously would have gone to the capitalists now goes to the workers. Thus there is a very strong case that anarchism makes workers much more free than any form of capitalism ever could since the workers are not subject to the whims of anyone else and get everything that they produce. This argument can seem very conclusive unless it is confronted with a few specific arguments.

The first thing that needs to be mentioned is that under an anarchistic society each individual worker could possibly even have less control over his own life. This is because the means of production are owned democratically and not by individual workers. This results in an economic order where each worker is subject to other workers instead of being subject to capitalists, this is not necessarily a more desirable outcome for any individual worker. And furthermore, since anarchism implies a democratic allocation of the resources within distinct industries, it also means that it stumbles onto the problems with large-scale democracies. There will be certain interest groups that will dominate the democratic relations and there will be less influence by individual workers as the interest groups hold the power within themselves.

This cannot be avoided whilst still having democratic control over the means of production. But still, as the majority will decide how the means of production should be utilized based on compromise, we may then jump to the conclusion that the individual worker has more control over the means of production. And thus the worker also has more control over his own life as his input becomes valuable in his own enterprise. This is not the case, in a capitalist system the worker always has to work for a capitalist and in the anarchist system, a worker always has to be a part of a democratically organized workplace. There is no more free choice in anarchism than there is in capitalism as workplace democracy is no more free for the people who are subject to it than capitalistic relations.

This may seem counterintuitive, after all, democracies in the real world are supposedly freer than monarchies, but this is not necessarily the case. The fact that each person can input their own opinion does not mean that they have any more of a choice when the king functions according to the desires of his subjects it is better for everyone than a compromise that everyone tolerates but no one actually wants. In a capitalist system, the capitalists have to try to attract the best workers, in an anarchist system, workers have barely any control over their lives as anarchism aims for an egalitarian distribution of resources. A worker cannot better themselves and gain a position of prominence, a worker can only move from one job to another, all of which are organized democratically and where they can never ascend to a higher position.

Thus we have to only prove that the capitalist has more of an incentive to create a workplace that caters to the workers more than a democratic process of decision making and we are on our way to demonstrating that capitalism can be freer than socialism even for the working class. It can be said that this is only an argument when we take our premise that freedom means productive choices and it could be that our premise is flawed. However, this would still be as much of an argument even without the premise, because workers must work in a democratically organized workplace under anarchism. It wouldn't demonstrate how workers are more free under capitalism, but it would demonstrate how workers are better off under capitalism. And to top it off I have seen very few anarchists who are willing to let workers decide to organize hierarchically and form capital relations and I have seen a comparably small amount of libertarians who are against workers organizing socialistically. Thus even if anarchism was not institutionally enforced, the workers would still lack a choice as the anarchists in that society would not let the workers organize capitalistically.

There needs to be some way to demonstrate whether democratic organization or capitalistic organization is more beneficial for the workers. Here we can bring in, as the conclusive argument, the commodification of labour socialists love to flaunt. Since labour is commodified under a capitalist system as the workers do not have direct control over how the fruits of their labour are utilized, their labour must also be similarly commodified under an anarchist system as the democratic unit has control of the labour of individual workers. We must establish whether this labour as a commodity is more valuable to the capitalist or the democratic organizational structure. This is if we want to establish whether a capitalist or an anarchist society will look out for the interests of each individual worker. And here we must contend that the profit produced by the worker is more valuable to the capitalist than the use value to the democratic unit which the worker is a part of. Workers may get collectively slightly longer breaks and better working conditions, but it is at the expense of each individual worker and their interest because the democratic unit has no reason to care about any individual worker.

Small-scale production may be undertaken democratically and when the democratic unit is very small, anarchism could work. However, since there is a need for consumer goods that require immense capital structures to establish prosperity, the democratic structures must be far-reaching. The capitalist aims to maximize the output of labour as when that is the case the capitalist benefits the most, this means that the capitalist must do all he can to preserve the quality of labour in his enterprise. And we can see this historically, many achievements that labour unions take credit for were actually implemented by capitalists expecting to profit more from having their workers work in better conditions.

And now we reach the question of the freedom for each worker to spend their money in the capitalist system or get access to resources based on use in the anarchist system. The first thing that we have to mention is that there will necessarily be a higher degree of scarcity in consumer goods in an anarchist society, this is not up for contention. This is simply because of the fact that workers are incentivized to work the least amount they can when organized democratically and have the highest standards when it comes to their workplaces. This is just the group interest of workers, all workers want to work less and all workers want to work in better conditions. This means that a lot of resources otherwise spent on production will be spent on making workplaces more enjoyable. This is a question whether anarchists value this more than having an "excessive" amount of consumer goods as is the case in a capitalist system.

This is not compensated by the additional value that capitalists otherwise would have taken from the economy. Even if we assume that the top 20% in society is the capitalist class and then if we assume that the workers get all the income from the capitalist class, they will only have doubled the amount of resources available to them. This may seem like a great amount of wealth available, but all the work done by the top 20% will then fall onto all the workers who got that additional income. And most of the top 20% are senior employees, extremely intelligent or highly trained. This is a guaranteed way to achieve less total wealth in society for each worker, in the absolute best case scenario everything evens out and the living standard does not either rise or fall with this redistribution. This is because the best estimate we can make here is the Pareto rule, which establishes that the top 20% do 80% of the work. The only percentage for which this redistribution would make sense is if only the top 2% was targeted, those are the richest of the rich. In this case, each person could expect around a 25% increase in their income without many labour-intensive societal duties being neglected. The only occupations in which there could be scarcity are extremely specialized positions in medical fields. When we still account for the additional costs that were previously covered by these people that now have to be covered by everyone else, this increase in income even at face value does not make much sense. The richest of the rich are the people who fund production to a large degree.

The only way that there can be an increased amount of income for the workers is if industries that do not provide use value are abolished. This is an argument that cannot properly be countered as there really could be more use value in the economy. But we also need to realize that these industries that do not produce use value exist to make money and thus if they were to disappear it would not free up labour to increase use value but rather decrease the value that the other goods had. Making money does not rely on arbitrary distribution or a generalized brainwashing, to earn money one has to make others value their goods more than they did previously when compared to costs. This necessitates an increase in the quality of the goods or the allocation of capital in a more efficient manner.

This is true even if we assume that use value is a proper measurement of economic well-being, we must still concede that on an individual level, each person does not value goods by their usefulness but rather their individual benefit. Capitalists increase their profits by increasing the benefit of their goods as compared to their costs or increasing the efficiency in their own enterprise or in the generalized economy. The lack of these functions will result in not just a state of increased use value but a state of roughly equal, if not less, subjective value. It may be true that people get more food and more clothes, but people will not get those things that they themselves want, the production of these goods will have reduced efficiency and the goods themselves will be of lesser quality.

Furthermore, the incentives to work high-intensity jobs that give the individual a lot of responsibility will be greatly reduced with no way to save and invest money or live in increased luxury. Thus, there should be no expectation of a general rise in social wealth but rather a decrease. Even at face value, each worker does not get much more than what he can consume. We can now say that if rent for land is no longer charged that workers would have that much more resources, but this is another assumption that does not make much sense. Land would still have to be allocated and what was previously land rents would have to become costs for what are now alternative means of allocating land. The only real parts where money would be gained with a transition to an anarchist society from the current one is where there previously was governmental restriction, which radical libertarianism also seeks to abolish.

Even in a perfect scenario, it's hard to see how the system of anarchy can cause an increase in societal wealth and this should not matter since the anarchists do not care about economic efficiency when contrasted by personal freedom. However, we have to consider whether people themselves having more resources may make them freer. When people have more options of what to do with their labour and are less bound by scarcity, there would surely be an increase in freedom and not a decrease in freedom as people would find themselves with more choices and more paths that they can take in life.

Since anarchism cannot provide this by any reasonable measure, it seems as if libertarianism is better at providing additional choices to do productive things with one's own labour. This is furthermore reinforced by the fact that the self-decency of every man will by necessity cause a structure of organization that is not as corruptly hierarchical as the current corporate one provided that there were actually free markets. We cannot imagine that people allowed free choice in organization and employment would choose to be in corporate structures or structures resembling corporate structures. Thus libertarianism, even though maintaining the relations between capital and worker, would not maintain the structure of those relations that are seen in the modern economy.

And furthermore, in the capitalist system production is for profit, this means that every niche will have goods produced for them as long as they desire those goods and are willing to pay for those goods. When production is for use there is by necessity a reduction in the quality and diversity of goods as goods are meant to be produced for direct consumption and not for producing profit to the capitalist. In capitalism, only one person has to decide that he wants to start an enterprise, in socialism, a great multitude has to provide their consent. As such, there will be less choice when it comes to the array of goods each person can access and there will be less general diversification of production.

Resources will not be allocated by private individuals in private transactions unless there is a very specific system of market anarchism. This will mean that each individual will have less choice in the goods he himself can obtain and not only the type and quality of the goods but also the category of the goods. It will be harder to find goods that are not local and that are not desired by many, this means that there will be perpetual shortages of goods that are not abundant in the region and for which there is no abundant demand in that region. Since each person does not transact for profit and since they have no ultimate control over the allocation of goods and the allocation of goods must be done via wider social structures, there will be ultimately less freedom in consumption.

The form of organization in the capitalist society is the rule of the consumers, the profit of the capitalist is only derived by providing what the consumers want to buy. In a capitalist society, each person has supreme command as long as they are the consumer. This does not imply a system of consumerism, but rather that the consumers have full choice over what they consume. In an anarchist society, the rule is by producers as production is not done to benefit those who consume. Since there is no profit, there can be no benefit for producing what others will consume and the producers will reign supreme. This may seem liberating, each person is freed in their work while sacrificing their freedom in consumption, but we must realize that work is done exclusively for consumption. The freedom in work does not mean that the worker is free, it only means that the work is more futile.

And finally, there is the matter that in a libertarian society any person answers to no other person unless they themselves associate with those people of their own free will. In an anarchist society each person must answer to the entirety of the society as the anarchist society does not internalize profits or costs. Anyone wanting to start an enterprise or live in alternative and unpopular ways must answer to the community as whole to be able to achieve their desired sort of life. In a libertarian society each person has to internalize all their costs and can internalize all their profits. Each person can live in any way they want without answering to anyone unless they themselves choose to do so. And there is a much broader array of allegiances in a libertarian society as there are no bars to any type of association as long as it is non-violent.

Although this argument is ineffective against anarchists, we can assert that there is no freedom at all unless property is protected, this is simply because for there to be freedom there has to be a way for which each person has the ability to make personal choices. When there is no way to make choices over property without having to mediate disputes, people do not have any freedom at all, when all property is owned by society as a whole it will be constantly under dispute. Since that property will be constantly subject to dispute, there is no freedom in a meaningful way for any individual as they cannot decide how property is used and will have to rely on what other persons decide to do with that property. Thus property rights are the only thing that can give people the freedom to do what they themselves want with any property.

II – Imperialism

Probably one of the most unfair criticisms of capitalism is that it always incentivizes one form of imperialism or another, as the capitalist class needs perpetually more territory to exploit. But this is still a seemingly hard notion to defeat as it stands on solid logic, if you have access to greater amounts of land and labour you can create greater profits and as such the capitalist class will strive to obtain control over as much land and labour as they can. The capitalists do this in order to create a system where they can obtain the largest amount of profit. If capitalist profits are derived from exploitation, the only way to increase profits is imperialism. Then to illustrate this the anarchists point out imperialism as perpetrated by the East India Company alongside other examples of colonial powers outsourcing imperialism.

The anarchists ignore the entire fact that the mercantilist economic system was wholly unlike the capitalist system where enterprise was not for private profit but for the benefit of the state. The East India Company also held a government granted monopoly which allowed it to institute the colonial rule in India. Chartered corporations have always been and do continue to be state appointed functionaries. This is completely unlike the free market which, in theory, should be completely devoid of government-sanctioned monopoly and where companies should function for profit and not so as to increase state power.

When confronted with this, the anarchists say that capitalism still inherently requires constant expansion and it doesn't matter what specific political structures are in effect. Without constant expansion, capitalism would be unable to sustain itself. To prove this the anarchists show the rise of multinational corporations and the working conditions they argue are sub-par in third world nations which are being exploited by foreign corporations. They assume that this is proof enough that capitalism is inherently imperialistic and that there can be no capitalism without having a tendency towards the centralization of power. There has seemingly never been a market economy without the exploitation of other countries and their resources. This is a very effective argument due to the simplistic nature and seemingly unbeatable nature. You can't argue against any point in the reasoning so it seems like you can't with the conclusion.

Capitalists do use third world countries to hire workers for lower wages than what they would have to provide for first world labour. Capitalist countries have been very imperialist in the past with the British Empire and currently, the imperialism exhibited by modern American foreign policy. And it's also undeniable that the more available resources capitalists have, the more they can expect to profit, especially when the resources are available for cheap in the third world as there are no developed markets in the third world. Furthermore, it's not like capitalists themselves have never engaged in violence to retain power in a foreign country. There are multiple examples of suppressing labour strikes in third world countries when that would have been unviable in first world countries. This sort of violence seemingly only demonstrates the imperialism inherent in capitalism.

The first argument before we get to the main argument is that for capitalists the best way to improve their own wealth is trade rather than domination. Practically, capitalists do not need to bear the costs involved in political rule if they can just contract freely without any coercion involved. When capitalists are allowed to contract freely, they will always choose trade over domination, as domination can only maximally produce the same benefits as trade can. Expanding markets is as profitable for the capitalist class as creating corporate power is. The capitalists may contract with people who do use coercion, but themselves investing into coercion is just a waste of capital. Capitalists would almost always rather refrain from imperialism if they can instead have free trade. Any singular capitalist would benefit more from imperialism than from free trade, however, this would be undesirable for other capitalists.

But the argument is framed from a perspective which can only lead to the conclusion of imperialism. This is the methodology of judging different states by their nature and not by a measure which looks at the other factors that go into imperialism. The premise of anarchist theory is that true socialism is stateless while capitalism must be violently imposed. This means that any imperialist actions of any state can be traced back to capitalist influences as the capitalist ruling class is necessarily in control of the state. Combined with empirical evidence of capitalists performing imperialism and the profit-seeking actions of the military-industrial complex, it is very easy to trick anyone into thinking that the problem is with capitalism.

The framing of the state as the executor of the capitalist class interest is enough for this theory to be accurate. Thus we need to deconstruct this notion and examine whether or not the state, by nature, is a part of the capitalist system or that capitalist systems need to be enforced by the state. We need to take two different definitions of the state and of capitalism to properly see where the different perspectives are coming from and which perspective approaches the truth. First, we can define the state as either any agency that enforces property law in a society, this seems fairly reasonable when we approach the world from an anarchist perspective. We can also define the state as any agency that monopolizes violence in some certain territory. Secondly, we can define capitalism as either a system of class domination by the capitalist class or a system of property rights and free enterprise. We are left with four combinations and we need to examine the merits of each of these definitions.

First, we can use the commonplace anarchist definition, that the state is an agency that enforces property, which anarchists think amounts to violence and also that capitalism is a system of class domination by the capitalist class. Since capitalism is class domination by the capitalist class and the state is the agency that enforces property, capitalism must be inherently exploitative as the dominant class uses the state to enforce property rights to maintain their domination. It would also be unavoidable that the state controls other facets of life other than simply property as the dominant class is directly interested in the state as the state is the one thing keeping their hegemony and shielding them from the natural, harmonious socialism which lacks all class distinctions and property rights.

The second is the classical libertarian minarchist definition, the state is the agency that protects property rights and capitalism is a system of property rights and free enterprise. This must result in a view that the state is essential to capitalism, however, that the capitalists can not justifiably hold any direct influence over the state as that would defeat the purpose of capitalism. This is the rhetoric you often hear from right-wing neo-liberals and objectivists, here we must also admit that imperialism is not caused by capitalism as the active involvement of the capitalists within the state goes contrary to capitalism and thus creates a wholly different system.

Then we can take the more authoritarian socialist[15] conception of the state and of capitalism. Capitalism being the domination by the capitalist class and the state as an agency of monopolized violence. This means that when there is a capitalist state, which is a state that is directly involved in the capitalist system, it will inherently fall to the whims of the capitalists. However, this is not a necessity for either capitalism and the state. From these premises, you can't really construct an argument that capitalism inherently leads to imperialism even if capitalism in itself is immoral. The state is a monopolist of violence so even while the capitalists are immoral, they only require the active permission of the state and not the explicit involvement of the state. The state only defends

---
15   This encompasses the right wing of socialism and the left wing of fascism.

property rights as far as that falls into the interest of the state and capitalists are as much subject to the whims of the state as all other people are. Furthermore, the authoritarians assume that the capitalist system needs to be dismantled by this sort of state and that they need to institute another system without class domination.

And finally there is the "anarcho"-capitalist approach which defines capitalism as a system of property and free enterprise and the state as a violent monopoly on force. This goes directly contrary to the notion that capitalism causes the state to be imperialistic and even reinforces the notion that capitalism and the state can't properly coexist so there is no theoretical possibility of a purely capitalist state. The state always needs to go against property rights and as such could never be capitalist, properly defined, and capitalism can't use the state as that would also violate property rights.

This means that if we manage to overthrow either the assumption that capitalism is a system of capitalist class domination or that the state is just any agency that protects capitalist property rights, the case that capitalism causes imperialism becomes incoherent. This reframes the argument in a fashion that the actions that create the imperialism must be caused by states and their interaction with capitalism and not the inherent codependence of capitalism and the state. Thus proving that the fact that capitalists being involved in imperialism could just as well be because the state incentivizes this behaviour and not because capitalists incentivize imperialism in states.

There may be a great deal of collaboration between the state and the capitalist class, but the capitalist class can't be at the root of the problem, we can even demonstrate this with all the common examples of imperialist capitalism. First, that the capitalists exploit the resources of third world nations to enrich themselves. This would cease to be true as capitalists would not be the main determinants of the third world nations if the problem was really with the capitalists. This means that either the profiteering from the third world is not exploitative as it is welcomed by the native people, or that the government of the nation invited the capitalists to profiteer off their countries for their own personal enrichment. Simply stopping the illusion that capitalists are behind all actions of the state will result in this being completely recontextualized. If capitalists do not necessarily hold permanent institutional power, it must be either the state that lets the natives down or no exploitation is necessary.

The other argument is that capitalists need to centralize and expand and this is why multinationals are formed. This too would be put into perspective provided we corrected our assumptions if capitalists were in control of the state this would be obviously the best strategy for individual wealth accumulation. However, if there was no direct connection between capitalism and the actions of the state we can assume that the state pushes capitalists to centralize and form multinationals as that benefits the state by allowing it to exercise more influence. This is no longer an essential tendency in capitalism but the result of the power-hungry nature of those who are in charge of the state. And an argument could be made that capitalists need to expand to get more resources as infinite growth could not be sustained on finite resources, but this ignores the growth of capital goods, knowledge and the economization of existing resources. Capitalists can grow further by creating more capital goods in the form of more efficient technology or utilizing existing capital goods in a more efficient way once they gain new knowledge. Capitalists could also profit from simply allocating resources in a better manner.

The only thing left to do is to provide enough arguments that the definitions for the state and capitalism can be shifted towards a direction that makes it possible to recontextualize the nature of capitalism and the state. The first thing we need to establish with the state is that the argument we currently have must only extend to the historical era of industrialism and all pre-industrial evidence is null. This is because in socialist theory the material conditions created different conclusions which did not need to favour capitalism before the industrial revolution. Thus, to make the argument harder and more persuasive we should also say that the 20th-century experiments in socialism were not socialist enough, that these did not properly abolish the property relations within society and as such still included a degree of capitalism. Under these conditions, we have to provide an argument that the state is not necessarily an agency of capitalist class domination.

Here we can provide a historical argument in the form of the progressive era in the united states as the best example that is also widely known. No person in their sane mind would argue that capitalist class domination was not reduced in the progressive era by the different reforms when compared to the gilded era before that time period. And this was not in the form of socialistic changes in the relations to property but rather simply using the state to acquire different privileges from the capitalists. If the capitalists were in charge of the state, this major populist uprising would not be able to happen unless it was directly and consistently socialist. It didn't try to abolish capitalism, but it reduced the amount of capitalism in society. It didn't change the material class character of the state, but it reduced capitalist influence. Since progressivism was not socialist, it should be impossible for it to have provided an opposition to the capitalist state. But it was neither socialist nor did it use the state for capitalistic purposes. The other experiments in the 20th century attempted to reach socialism, so it can easily be argued that the reduction of the power of capitalists under them was a direct result of socialistic practice counteracting the capitalist state. This is not the case with progressives, there can be no argument made that the state was not responsible for a reduction of property rights and an increase in the power of the middle and working classes.

Then there is the philosophical argument when it comes to protecting property. If we define the state as any agency that protects property we would have to include private forces, we can also stipulate that these private forces must be truly private and not have a state licence thus excluding all modern examples of private defence. Since any agency that protects property is the state, then if that agency was devoid of politics, it would just be an autocratic dictatorship and act as such. This notion would effectively debunk any ideology that strives towards a stateless capitalism and it is constantly used in that context. But this is not the case in any real market.

The argument for why this is not so is extremely long, but the condensed version simply states that the universal access to providing defence ensures that no one defence agency can go unchecked as the other defence agencies could profit from suppressing any agency that goes against the interests of the public. Since the provision defence is decentralized, as there is no singular agency that holds the moral and legal right to provide defence, there is no way in which an agency can dominate the market in such a manner that would suppress all competition. Thus it is much better to coexist and do business in a reasonable manner as all other industries aside from defence do and not form any sort of dictatorships, this is the same reason why even the most imperialist country has never been able to achieve anything close to effective and totalitarian world domination.

And we can even historically back this theory too, which should conclusively prove that all agencies that protect property rights do not need to be the state. In the American Frontier, there were many agencies that were independent from the state which protected mostly their own property. Even though the frontier was under the jurisdiction of the federal government, local defence was handled by different local groups with no affiliation with the state. This did not result in massive chaos and we cannot say that any effective defence of property rights requires the state, as the so-called Wild

West was relatively tame compared to many states in history[16]. Even if the image of the frontier may be gunslingers and bandits, the usual operations were very peaceful even during heated occasions. Of course the Wild West is not the only place in which private defence has ever functioned[17], but it is the most relevant example.

All this should make it fairly conclusive that theoretically, it is possible to protect property rights without the state without it necessarily devolving into a state. Even though there could not be a state that didn't at least protect the property rights of itself, this does not make any agency that protects property rights a state. If everyone who protected property rights was a state, we would have to assume that individuals acting in self-defence become states. If only institutional protectors of property rights are states, then we must also concede that any revolutionary activity that aims to topple the existing state without instituting communism has already become a state without gaining access to legitimized compulsion. Both of these are fairly absurd assumptions and it should not be true that any protector of property rights is automatically a state.

The two conceptions of capitalism are backed by their own supporters and detractors, first, there is the notion that capitalism

---

[16]

    For more information, I suggest reading "The Not So Wild, Wild West".

[17]

    An important objection to tackle is that private defence has only ever functioned due to not being at war with a central state. But this is the same as saying that the police only function due to gangs choosing not to commit murder, which is similarly nonsensical.

simply describes a system of capitalist class domination. This is based on socialist theory which describes capitalism as exclusively a system of coercion. Since socialist theory popularized the term capitalism, it is reasonable to concede that socialist theory has some bearing on what the word capitalism means. Even though this may be the more accurate definition of capitalism, no one actually defends this form of capitalism and the supporters of capitalism are really defending free enterprise and property rights. There may be people who aim to fuel class conflict or enrich themselves by furthering the domination of the capitalist class, but they are usually only pragmatic and not ideological. They are defending themselves and not a consistent economic system. The supporters of capitalism want to create strong property rights and a system of free enterprise, so to say that their goal is capitalist class domination is simply disingenuous. The question then becomes whether property rights and free enterprise are synonymous with capitalist class domination or whether capitalist class domination goes contrary to property rights and free enterprise.

It would be easy to make both cases, the first we can simply say that the inherent inequality in free enterprise and the ownership of property will create a higher class of privileged people who can exploit the lower class as they control the economy. This means whenever property is protected and enterprise is allowed to remain free, there will be capitalist class domination. But this is somewhat contradictory as everyone can gain access and lose access to property and everyone can start their own enterprise. The fact that in reality, this does not happen is not an argument against the potential ability to own property and a business.

The fact that some people are successful while others aren't could also show that capitalism selects the best people to be in charge of the vastest amount of wealth. This means wealth under capitalism would be best allocated to the most useful ventures. Furthermore, we can't necessarily assume that owning capital is a privilege or a personal benefit, the profits that come from capital are obviously preferred to having no profits and most people would theoretically have more capital than less capital. But in practical terms capital is a very expensive liability. This is because the question is not between capital and no capital, but capital and stable investment vehicles such as money, consumer goods or real estate. Capital needs to be perpetually managed and maintained if one expects to profit off of it. We must find a way to solve this conflict between the two positions that both hold merit.

When people have capital, they trade ease of mind and a stability of resources for an enterprise which needs constant attention. But the capital owners are able to profit provided that they manage their capital well and can obtain economic power. Furthermore, capital is heavily needed in any economy and as such capitalists would be in a position of eminence if they can offer well managed and maintained capital. The question ultimately becomes whether inequality is always a detriment to the quality of life for the people who are not in the higher class and whether or not humans all deserve equality. This is a question of whether the responsibility of capital ownership entitles the capitalists to a higher hierarchical position. Furthermore, there is the distinct possibility of a scenario in which a capitalist might completely lose their personal fortune provided that market conditions become unfavourable.

However, the supporters of capitalism have answered these questions in very succinct and convincing manners. First, since in a free market people are allowed to contract, there can be no inherent domination as workers are free to refuse to be exploited by capitalists. It would leave them to fend for their own and it would restrict their access to capital, however, the exploitation is preferred to surviving without this capital. Only once free markets are restricted does exploitation become inherent in capitalism.

When someone is left to starve because they can't feed themselves, it's not the consequence of the capitalists refusing to feed him but rather the consequence of the actions that he himself took that caused him to be unable to gain access to food. Since he made decisions that removed the ability to eat, he himself is the only party to blame for any lack of food he may experience. However, when the access to capital is not made artificially expensive by the state and when capital is not made more valuable without increasing in quality, the state is to blame for resulting unemployment and economic coercion. This is a brutal view, but we must remember that having to guarantee your own food and shelter does not preclude that others cannot willingly and freely offer food and shelter.

Thus the issue is not inherent in capitalism but rather inherent in reality, the problem is not that hierarchies are bad for the people who are at the bottom, even though they would prefer to be at the top. One can contend this by saying that if capitalists do not refuse to give workers access to capita,l workers would be able to make money and provide for themselves, thus the capitalists are still at fault. But this assumes that access to capital is a fundamental part of reality and society. But if accessing capital was a fundamental part of reality, workers would not need capitalists to provide them with capital. If access to capital is a fundamental part of society, there would be no need to abolish property as each person would be willingly allowed the use of capital. As long as capitalists can't coerce the workers, the workers could gain access to capital from the supposedly abundant resources that there are which would make it a part of nature to have access to capital.

There is again a valid objection in the form of pointing out that other workers created this capital and the capitalists only paid them wages. However, if this is the case and there is nothing more behind it, there is no problem with capitalism as workers would be able to build capital all on their own and the only problem with exploitation is still that workers choose to get exploited. The only reason why workers do not become self-sufficient must be because getting exploited is better than other alternatives, there is no inherent exploitation, or that state or private violence prevents workers from being independent. Thus the focus should be on eliminating private violence and the state which do not allow workers to organize as they please and not blame scarce capital for personal problems.

The second part of this question is whether humans deserve equality or not, whether the state of being human should give a person access to what is considered to be their human rights. Are there a class of essential things that should be equally available to all without charge for the sake of basic human decency? But here again, we are facing the sad fact that there is nothing natural or inherent to being human about this sort of equality. We care for our fellow man and seek to provide our aid, but we live in scarcity and as such we cannot expect there to be freely available goods. Humans don't deserve financial or material equality as there is no inherent equality in being human. Humans deserve compassion, but the provision of this compassion should be left to an individual basis and not one that is systematic. The moral equality of humans does not mean that it is possible to properly morally realize some notion of human rights that would give people access to basic amenities. And if socialism is really contingent on having basic necessities abundantly provided to all, it could be realized in a pure market economy by active participation in a community.

And this is reflected in economic truth, whenever something is available for free, people are incentivized to try to use it if they are able to. The fundamental preference, discounting morals, is for owning goods rather than not owning goods. If scarce goods are distributed without charge, people will seek to gain access to as many of these goods as possible. This means that due to the scarcity of these goods there will be shortages and misallocations. Furthermore, they will be misused as people do not need to bear any personal cost to obtain these goods. We can't reasonably distribute goods without cost while expecting them to be effectively used.

We would have to here conclude that capitalism is not inherently a system of exploitation, rather capitalism is the best we can do at worst. Capitalism could theoretically still be imperfect, but it is the natural result of economizing scarce resources and capitalists are not just dominant because they are capitalists. It is not necessarily synonymous with violent exploitation and oppression. However, if there is any involvement of the state, the system of capitalism can easily deteriorate into an oppressive system. This is not some innate tendency of capitalism, but an innate tendency in the state to seek as much power as it can.

The final objection to this is that we could be living in superabundance if we automated as much as we could. This is the post-scarcity anarchism where supposedly the existence of the possibility to feed everyone is proof enough that we no longer need capitalism and can abolish that entire system. But capitalism created the entire system that allowed for the elimination of relative scarcity, if we want to decrease scarcity even further, the answer should be more capitalism. We could live in a relatively abundant condition if nothing was ever produced beyond what is produced right now, but we could live so much better if we allowed capitalism to work further. This is because in a proper capitalist system we would be able to obtain an even more widespread and effective access to consumer goods as more economic development increases the prosperity in society as a whole. As such we would find ourselves in relative abundance with little effort in a short amount of time if we allowed for further capitalism and not for an abolition of the capitalist system.

If either capitalism is not inherently coercive or the state is inherently coercive, then it can't be that capitalism and the state are inherently tied together as capitalism and the state would be distinct and separate entities and would not work to serve each other. This means that the imperialist actions of various states would not be the imperialist actions of capitalism and it would ensure that capitalism is not the cause of imperialism. But rather, the state can use capitalism in order to advance its own imperialism. The logic that the capitalists are behind the economic and political imperialism that is taking place is congruent on the assumption that the purpose of the state is to serve the capitalist class by protecting them.

There is one final argument to demonstrate how the state becomes more imperialistic as it allows for more capitalism if we assume that capitalism produces material prosperity. Which is only reasonable to do as capitalism is in large part based on each person maximizing their own material prosperity. Then we can assume that the state by taxing can increase its own wealth. Since the capitalist state can rapidly increase its own wealth with the growth of the economy, it can then strive to gain further influence and now can fund imperialism with the excess wealth produced by capitalism. In this way, it's not that capitalism creates imperialism, but rather wealthy nations become imperialist and capitalism is able to create wealthy nations which the state is able to use to build an empire.

III – Statism

A common critique of a completely free market system is that it's inherently statist, no matter what one might do, the rich will hold greater access to violence and thus will domineer over the poor in society. From this, it is possible to infer that being against the state requires being against capitalism since capitalism requires a state to maintain itself. There is also the argument that property rights need to be enforced by the state, but this is easy to defeat. The state is not special in any other way than that it holds legitimized violence, all the duties of the state can be delegated to private actors. This means that everything the state had a monopoly on can be transferred to private parties with no such monopoly. Since there is no more monopoly on defending property rights, no new state is formed. It may seem like it is a form of governance when private entities can enforce some form of law, but they do not have institutional and monopolized violence, so it can't be considered inherently statist.

The second reason why capitalism needs a state is derived from the first, this is that class structures with property rights necessitate that there be a monopoly on violence to suppress the oppressed working class and to ensure that the capitalists can get their profits from the surplus value produced by the workers. It's not that there can never be private police and that the police will by necessity be oppressive, but rather that the class structure within a capitalist society requires an oppressive police to uphold. Thus you can have anarchist defence and defence without the state, but this defence cannot exist while there are class distinctions within society. Here we must get into what class distinctions are to further examine this subject.

Marxist social theory supposes that there are always different groups with conflicting interests and that one of those groups is at a dominant position over the other, this is unless full communism is reached where all classes are abolished. In the same manner in which the feudal lord held a dominant position over the serf, a capitalist holds a dominant position over the worker. The ruling class is in one way or another privileged over the class that is being ruled, there is inherent oppression within any system that has class differences. Because of this, the only system in which there is no oppression is one where there are no class distinctions and vice versa. Using this theory, the system of capitalism must inherently have a way in which the ruling capitalist class can gain dominion over the ruled working class.

For this to be possible, the property relations within capitalism must be defined in such a way that the capitalist class benefits while the labouring class is exploited. Anarchists claim that this applies to all structures of property rights as long as these structures defend private property. And to an extent this makes sense, workers would be better off if they could just walk into any factory and didn't have to pay capitalists for the use of their capital. In this manner, it must be that the system where workers are unable to get the best treatment they could, is a system of coercion. And only the state can sustain coercion for long periods of time, so capitalism must require the state in order to maintain capitalist domination over the workers. For there to be private property, the entirety of society must be forced under a legal system that is based on defending private property. This system of law holds private property above other moral values and the laws must be enforced coercively within this ethical assumption. Whenever there is capitalist law and there is organized defence for that law and as long as that law defends the class structure which privileges the capitalist, there must be a state. If there was no state, property rights could not be maintained.

The law could not privilege the capitalist and protect the private property of that capitalist without the state, this is simply because the definition of the state would ensure that there can be no private property without the state. In this form, those who advocate for a stateless capitalism are caught in a trap. Either they have to ignore this argument and try to railroad it and claim that it isn't the state if someone else does it or become admitted socialists or statists. The first argument that can be made is easy, we can just suppose there are no meaningful class distinctions within a free market and property is more accessible so capitalism is also beneficial for the working class. We can also say that since people are free to leave and establish their own societies there is no such violent hegemony. This is not true right now as the state stops people from forming their own societies, however, if the state would be replaced by decentralized law and voluntaryist principles, there would be no stopping of anarchists who wanted to live without capitalism. Both of these arguments can be effective when framed properly, but they are answering questions other than the one asked.

There is still the notion that to prevent the underprivileged class from revolting there is a need for coercion. To properly disprove this we have to either prove that humans are naturally just, we believe in equal protections for people who go contrary to their interest. Or we need to prove that humans are naturally servile, we are ready to accept lower positions as we believe we do not inherently deserve more. In this form, we either have to prove natural tendencies towards strict hierarchy or natural tendencies towards equality under the law without material equality[18].

If humans are naturally prone to hierarchy there does not need to be any violence to enforce the class distinctions within capitalism and if humans are naturally prone to justice they don't need to be compelled to respect the property of another. The anarchists will never believe that humans are naturally hierarchical, so I will leave the defence for that position for the end of this section but we need to now examine the notion of justice. This simply states that humans are willing to accept a detriment to themselves to have society organized in a way that is more just, this in a way ties into hierarchy, but not necessarily. Someone who belongs to the class that does not own property could defend the ownership of property because the ownership of property is

---

[18] This does not apply to other ingroup-outgroup conflicts. It is assuming that the dispute over property rights is happening within the sociologically defined ingroup. The outgroup of capitalists or workers is defined materially and not socially. Socially defined outgroups require a different theory if they are to be reconciled with the ingroup.

perceived as moral above the theft of property. I would make the case that to even advocate for a stateless society in any capacity requires belief in a certain degree of natural justice within humans.

A stateless society fundamentally implies a society in which voluntary interactions are valued above involuntary interactions. But the definition of what is voluntary differs between socialistic and capitalistic thought. We must also acknowledge that interactions which involve two or more people where any amount of compromise or economizing is necessary, can never be truly voluntary, in the socialist sense. This is if we are using the notion of something being voluntary as people freely accepting it and not preferring an alternative manner to solve the issue. In the case where people accept something unfreely, that is people are okay with something but only begrudgingly or out of duty, it is not voluntary in the way in which completely free acts are voluntary. In such a way one can make the case that, even though working for a capitalist is consensual, it is not voluntary as the worker is being pressured by fundamental economic conditions. Relations with any law are likewise also involuntary to some degree, one is unable to choose whether he will obey the law within a certain society or not. He is subject to the law which defines the social norms in which people interact in, but he was never given the right to choose the law.

Thus statelessness can never completely transcend the need for a degree of involuntaryism as there is no situation in which social agreements or norms are completely non-existent and people relate completely freely. This is impossible because the meaning of free interaction differs between individuals since the goals and wants of these individuals differ. No person can ever be truly satisfied whenever interacting with another person as people have different values and plans. Thus there are two solutions to the problem of law, either outright violence in which the problem is solved by combat and theft. Or institutional violence, in which the problem is solved by enforcing and creating social rules and norms in advance that are enforced through courts and police.

To believe in a stateless society you have to accept that even when you value the voluntary above the involuntary. When it comes to conflicts between people, you either have to choose between covert and overt force. If you strictly define involuntary actions as being only relevant when there is overt violence, you solve this problem. But this ignores the fundamental social condition and is not satisfactory for anarchists. Anarchists must find a way to ensure that the dispute over property management does not devolve in such a way that chaos is the perpetual state of man. When chaos becomes perpetual, violence in the form of theft and murder will become commonplace.

Thus to value a society based on voluntary interactions one has to value a society based on some degree of social norms and one has to believe that these social norms will be established in a just and fair manner. If people are willing to accept a degree of involuntaryism to avoid overt violence, there can be a stateless society that also has class structures. And we must rule out direct, physical violence because not only is it involuntary, it is also destructive and if we are to believe that we can have a society based primarily on voluntary interactions without the state we must figure that conflicts must be solved in some other manner. That is to believe in a stateless society we must believe that people are to some degree just.

And these conflicts will not only be conflicts of revenge, honour or passion. These conflicts will be to a large extent about the unharmonious allocation of resources where all resources are not allocated ideally to the interest of every person. This is because resources are scarce and conflicts between people relating to how they should be allocated will always be present until there is a superabundance of all goods. There will never be a superabundance of all goods unless the world changes so drastically that we can't even imagine how it could do so. There is and will be, at least for the foreseeable future, scarcity and as such conflict about how resources are to be allocated.

Since people have to be moral to some degree as that is necessary for any stateless society or anarchic society, we must also establish that this innate justice is conceptually enough to make people conform to rules that may be immediately detrimental. Even though it might technically privilege a certain class if private property is protected, it might not be oppressive as the innate justice within human society is enough to protect these norms to property. If this isn't the case, then all other stateless societies would be as impossible as a capitalistic one and there could be no chance for a stateless society. People need to have the ability to make compromises that are detrimental to them as long as there is scarcity and as long as there is no perfect harmony of interests. This is necessarily solved with overt or covert violence, we should prefer covert violence and the sense of justice that people have makes covert violence not oppressive as we are willing to accept it to not have overt violence[19].

The other argument is the notion that humans are fundamentally hierarchical. Anarchists reject this argument, but it is an argument that has to be mentioned. The basic argument against the feasibility of a stateless capitalism is the one presented above, but it relies on the notion that all class distinctions are oppressive to lower classes because the higher classes need to maintain their class distinction strictly by violence. This ceases to be the case when we consider the point that humans might naturally organize into classes and thus the lower classes do not try to break down the class distinctions of the upper classes and thus do not need to be suppressed.

In this regard, the workers would not rise up against the capitalists organically and only would ever do so once provoked. The one argument against this is really one from dialectics and tribal history, that is class distinctions have historically been continuously done away with. The other argument is that there was supposedly no hierarchy in tribal societies. Thus humans are necessarily not built for living in hierarchies. The first argument falls apart when we consider that the class distinctions that have been broken down have never been ones based on wealth and that wealth has always been a massive distinction between the classes

---

[19] This is not to be confused with statist forms of social contract theory that suppose that the only way to do so is to surrender our rights to the state.

of society. The class distinctions that have been broken down are always legal privileges that make the law apply differently to each person. Even though in a form the capitalistic society might be built on privilege inherent in the law that lets the capitalists own property, it is not built with legal distinctions[20].

In this manner, if we are to analyse history dialectically, we can not pin down the conflict to one where it is simply of material relations but rather to a conflict of legal relations. There has always been a struggle to get superior rights from the agency that is the state. This interpretation of dialectical history is more backed up by the actual historical analysis and not necessarily the one where we strictly look at the material relations in society. In this manner, the hierarchy of wealth may be completely natural to humans even though hierarchies within the legal system are often contested. If groups can obtain access to legal violence to benefit themselves, they will aim to do so, this creates an inherent conflict within any statist society.

The second argument is that tribal societies were in some manner egalitarian and thus there are no hierarchies inherent in the ways that humans organize. And this is true to an extent, in tribal societies the material relations are fairly egalitarian, but social relations are still strictly hierarchical. However, we have only had limited contact with undisturbed tribal societies for scientific inquiry. We may still draw the conclusion that from these facts tribal societies demonstrate how material differences are socially

---

[20] This is unless the state constructs a legal system which prioritizes wealth over justice, as is the case in many countries in the modern world.

constructed. Some people may have more than others, but no person can be distinguished by their economic role. This is simply contested by the fact that when we introduced these tribal societies to abundance, that is when these tribal societies obtained a massive increase in resources from trading with the white europeans who interacted with them, they created societies where there are differences in material equality. It is more likely that material equality was largely the result of material scarcity. This leads to the optimal strategy for economizing resources to be holding property in common. Thus we can draw the conclusion that humans are hierarchical even materially, however, when there is generalized extreme poverty, hierarchy cannot manifest itself[21].

---

[21]
    If this chapter feels incomplete because it focused on oppression as it relates to law and did not discuss whether or not property itself is oppressive, I would direct the reader to the chapters: "Real Estate", "Freedom", "Exploitation" and "Property".

IV – Property

The single most common objection to libertarian capitalism from libertarian socialists is the notion that private property requires a state to protect. Or that protecting property manifests itself as a state and thus is incompatible with libertarianism. There are two ways in which anarchists rationalize it[22], first, that there is a distinction between personal property and private property based on occupancy and use. The second rationalization asserts that excluding others from property that you necessarily have no need for, is incompatible with a free society. Most often you hear the first argument, however, I still feel the need to acknowledge the somewhat more obscure argument based on the need of others trumping the right to property.

Supposedly there are two classes of property, the first class is the property that people personally and continuously use, that is personal property. People supposedly have a right to this property because they gain the most utility out of it and continuously occupy it without renting it out to any other person. This personal property cannot be rented, if it was rented then other people would become both the primary users and the occupiers of this property. Any property that doesn't meet this simple qualification is not personal property but rather private property. In effect, if you have a moderate size house and if you want to retain your personal belongings, anarchists say that you are allowed to do that.

---

[22] In actuality there are quite a few other ways, these are tackled in other chapters and are not dealt with here.

However, when you accumulate excess you no longer have a right to it because someone else can occupy this property without any direct cost to you. This is a bit more technical than the moral argument you usually hear is, but I felt that this was necessary for a consistent standard of what is personal property.

Thus when someone can occupy your perceived property without any direct cost to you and when you are not the primary user of that prcperty, they are then in their complete rights to do so. In effect, if you own a factory, the workers you hired can seize it without any damage to your person. And as you only collect the profits from the factory and don't expend your labour in production, the workers can be thought of as the primary users of the factory. This is because they continuously put their labour into the factory and occupy a much larger share of the factory, even if your money is involved. The same sort of logic goes for any sort of excess or land ownership that is tied up in the enterprise that requires the labour of others to function. In essence, any property that you retain for your own use is property that doesn't require the main users and the occupiers of that property to be violently suppressed and as such, it is legitimate unlike the private property capitalists advocate.

And if we take this at face value we can really not argue with it, you do have to put down rebellion within the workers if you are to retain your factory. The workers really are the primary users of the factory and the workers do occupy the factory. In essence, it seems as if you need to use violence to perpetuate the system of capitalism as if you did not the workers would overthrow the capitalist class and take over the property that they already operate. There only is violence once the capitalists decide to suppress the worker insurrection, the insurrection itself would reduce violence in society. When property is owned commonly, no one needs to be suppressed from owning the property that they occupy and use. Thus, if you want to achieve a stateless society, it cannot fundamentally have private property. If it does have private property, it will require an agency of violence to enforce property rights across the entirety of society, thus constituting a state.

When we take this argument at face value it may seem ethically absurd, but when we take it on the premises that it itself set out, it seems to be a reasonable argument. Even though we may theorize about property acquisition, the argument seemingly makes a compelling point that capitalism is inherently violent. However, now we should introduce the theory that property ownership is violent as it excludes people from privately owned property even if they are in greater need of it, this is important to introduce because the answers to both questions are largely the same. Contrary to the previous argument this doesn't introduce a distinction between private and personal belongings but simply states that it is violent to withhold property from people who are in greater need for it. You much more often hear this in ordinary socialist circles and not used for the argument that capitalism needs a state, but this point is still made.

The argument holds that since capitalism withholds resources from people who have a greater need for these resources, capitalism must necessitate violence to remove the access to these resources from the people for whom it is vital to gain access to these resources. In this way, capitalism kills millions due to starvation and disease as it excludes the global poor from food, water, and the required medicine to treat illnesses. From this, it is possible to infer that the particular exclusion inherent in capitalism is the result of systematic violence, or in other terms the state enforcing capitalist property relations. Thus it needs to be the case that capitalism is inherently violent as if it wasn't, these needless deaths could be solved with other methods of property allocation, touted as also being more efficient.

We can first address the second argument from which we can address the first one. The problem with the argument is that it treats access to goods as a fundamental condition and not a condition built upon economic advancement. It treats prosperity as something that is there irregardless of whatever the capitalists do. It acts as if prosperity is free and that there is no charge to be paid if one is to have a prosperous society. If prosperity is not a natural phenomenon, it is not violent to deprive people of resources as these resources are not facts of nature, but rather conditions created artificially. Since these resources are artificially created, it is not violent to deny access to these resources as they should be used at the discretion of the person who created these resources. At least provided he created these resources without imposing any additional costs on anyone[23]. Thus the violence involved is simply

---

[23] Really wise guys can now seemingly catch me in a logical contradiction, the capitalist did impose costs on the workers! Aha! However, the capitalist also recuperated these costs, if he had not, then the workers would rather be jobless than work for a capitalist.

capturing the benefits from an additional increase in the living standard that the capitalist created himself.

And it was not the workers that made material conditions improve as work on its own cannot create anything. Work can only execute plans that are established and funded even before the work takes place. If these plans fail at producing prosperity, the capitalist must take a loss instead of a profit. Work can only follow a plan and the plan that this work follows is the plan that the capitalist sets. Workers do not create any value as the value workers create is only relevant insofar as they execute the vision of the entrepreneur and the capitalist. This vision is for which the capitalist and the entrepreneur are rewarded and it is a fundamental condition for creating prosperity. Without people who are able to innovate and plan, there can never be any prosperity and there can never be any advancement in human societies. Prosperity is only created by the people who create the plan that eventually creates prosperity, to do this it is necessary to stake the capitalists own wealth on the success of the plan. If they fail, they pay the costs, if they succeed, they reap the benefits in the form of profits.

Cpitalism didn't kill millions upon millions of people as it violently excluded them from resources using state power[24]. These people died from a lack of resources which is the natural condition of the world without capitalists. There can still be one objection and that is that society has fundamentally changed to an extent where abundance is the norm. By doing this, the person arguing

---

[24] Furthermore, it is amusing that the "deaths by capitalism" come overwhelmingly from countries that have leftist governments.

that capitalism is inherently violent can argue from the perspective that even though a thousand years ago starvation may have been the norm, modern material conditions have made it irrelevant. However, modern material conditions are too developed from those who improve upon the world, this is funded by the capitalists capturing the profits from their endeavours. We can take it at face value that prosperity would somehow stay the norm even if a drastic rearrangement in the relationship of material conditions were to occur. But this is not proof that there is such a fundamental increase in prosperity that the material conditions could provide everyone with excess and that removing this excess from someone is violent.

The last argument to be made is that the state of human knowledge is simply enough to change the fundamental nature of society. From that, we could hypothetically argue that capitalism is simply privatizing the knowledge in society and in that manner it is violent. Capitalism excludes people from wealth who are a part of the society whose knowledge capitalism privatizes. And although this is a good argument against copyright, it doesn't hold up against private property. If we take knowledge as a constant, there is no need to even change the capitalist society. If increased knowledge so fundamentally changes society that poverty can be eliminated and scarcity becomes an artificial construct, socialists should have already achieved their technological utopia. After all, the constant of knowledge should be enough to provide them with a lack of scarcity and thus could remove them from the capitalist society.

And this leads us to the first argument, we can not treat it as workers being suppressed on property they themselves have access to. But rather we need to see workers as having to gain access to the property to produce profits for the capitalists and earn wages for themselves. In this way, it is not as if the access to factories or big houses or whatever else is a fact of nature, but rather they are improvements built by the allocation of resources by certain individuals. It is true that it may be better for workers if they did not have to pay for access, but it is in no way violent to demand payment from the workers who desire access to the capital they themselves do not have. Workers could obtain access to capital without the intervention of any capitalist, but there are certain problems with that.

First, workers would not get paid before products are sold unless they manage to attract enough investment in resources to be able to pay themselves. This means that for socialistic organization to be feasible, the workers first need to get capital from someone and if they get it through stock or loans, it devolves into a different organizational structure in capitalism. This is not a perversity within capitalism, but rather the nature of life itself. If anyone wants to access property, they have to save money or pay people who have already built up capital stores. The only other ways are to either organize a group of workers who can themselves pay for the resources required to form capital or to violently seize the resources of others. And since the resources of others are not facts of nature, the seizing of these resources is indeed violent and not the recovery of something that belongs to workers. This is the role the capitalist or the investor plays in the capitalist society, they invest in the efforts of workers and set up managerial structures to ensure that this investment pays off. The profit of the capitalist is just the return on that investment that allows workers to earn a good living.

One can propose the counter-factual that no such problems would exist in a socialist economy, but there is still a need for resources and still a need for people who produce what used to be capital goods. The workers still need to collectively put together all goods needed for building up new ventures. Thus the people within the socialist economy still need to obtain access to resources, it's just a matter whether this access is planned by councils, decentralized mutual aid or gifts, the same problems are still present as in a capitalist economy. There is the additional issue of there being no incentive to invest in the efforts of others unless they directly benefit you. In a capitalist system the capitalist benefits from benefiting others, profit is entirely derived from sales and sales are derived from satisfying some want or need. Under anarchism, there is a system where the economy devolves into a pseudo-industrial version of agrarianism or state socialism where the state-equivalent allocates resources.

There is also another problem, that is that the risk of these ventures is wholly on the workers as there is no capitalist to assume the damages of a failed enterprise. This means that either the losses are socialized upon the entirety of the economy if they are derived from a common fund or they are losses upon the workers who started to undertake this new effort. In either scenario, there is a failure to incentivize the creation of new projects as there is no reward for risking your capital as resources are allocated to production for need and not production for profit. Thus anarchists devolve themselves either further into primitivism where creativity in creating new enterprise is stifled or they introduce an equivalent of state socialism to compel people to work. Even though anarchism is consistent in theory, when we introduce economic reality, it becomes an extremely naive worldview.

V – Commodity Production[25]

The problem of commodity production is shared between different brands of non-authoritarian socialism and anarchism, one of the objections these sorts of people have to capitalism is that capitalism produces commodities. Commodities are objects whose entire purpose is to be bought and sold instead of objects that are produced solely for the good of the society. It is held that commodity production is immoral as producing goods to be bought and sold goes against fundamental economic morality as it results in exploitation. If products are to be bought and sold, it must also be true that those who make these products are to be bought and sold. This is true because these products are made with the labour of the people who make them, as such any system of commodity production must also commodify the labour of individuals and cause a lack of self-ownership.

Furthermore, this commodity production does not take into account the social needs of the society but rather functions only based on profit and strives solely to make as much money as possible instead of creating as much good as possible. This is because capitalism allows for pricing goods beyond their use value and the value of the labour embodied in these goods resulting in the goods being sold for more than they would logically be worth.

---
[25] Throughout this essay and partially throughout the rest of the book I use the term "mutual aid' to refer to the philosophy of mutualism and I use "production for need" for the libertarian socialist concept of "production for use". Even though this is not common socialist vernacular, I use these words as I am writing primarily for a right-wing audience and they provide more context and clarity.

Supply and demand should not be seen, according to these people, as supply adjusting to create the most profit from catering to demand but rather demand itself should serve as a signal for creating more supply instead of raising prices. More authoritarian socialists still favour commodity production, they only want to create a socialistic system of producing commodities instead of capitalist commodity production. However, there is a tendency in anarchist circles to oppose the production of any and all commodities and instead only produce things that have use value and distribute these according to need.

This case seems weak to everyone not socialistically inclined as the production of commodities is such a fundamental part of life and to give this up would be absurd. However, when people are already inclined towards socialism, the notion that there should be no commodities produced, only strengthens the case for socialism and can be used to demonstrate how capitalism will inherently result in workers being seen as a lesser class than capitalists are. Furthermore, this demonstrates how capitalism will always allocate resources in an immoral way instead of allocating resources to those who need those resources. This fundamentally erases the importance of supply and demand as an economic concept. And this is done only for the sake of the profit for private entities with no social responsibilities other than making profit.

This is supposedly a conclusive demonstration of how there is no such thing as ethical capitalism as capitalism by necessity produces commodities. There are two plans to produce goods in forms that don't require commodity production that these socialists put forth. The first is the production for need, the second is mutual aid. Both systems are very similar, yet have differences that make the second possible economically and the first a complete impossibility. This is to say nothing about the effectiveness of all of these systems. First, we ought to tackle the ludicrous idea that the production within a society should be for need and not for any type of profit. The schemes proposed for this differ from anarchist to anarchist, but I will describe the most common one.

The moral argument for this is simple, each person has needs and each person has a quantity of labour they can put into the economy, thus each person can put an equal amount of effort into the economy (which means different quantities of labour) and receive the things that they need the most urgently. You can create a giant pool of goods and services to be distributed to those people who most require access to these goods and services. In theory, everyone could have their needs satisfied without having to put more effort into the economy than anyone else. Even though to some this may seem like a utopian idea, I would argue that it is neither utopian or practical. First, even if it worked perfectly, it would forcefully erase the distinctions between different people and would create a society in which different people would be treated similarly no matter what the quality of their labour is. This means that the people who are the aptest are punished for being apt and the neediest are rewarded for being needy, this is the most immoral system imaginable[26].

26
    Of course, for the neediest people who are not apt at all, this is a perfect system.

Furthermore, the immorality of the system also makes it impractical, since it punishes the able and rewards the unable. It results in there being less able people and more unable people, the theory that there could be production for need is just a childish delusion. Furthermore, there is no way to accurately measure who needs how much of what, there is no way to determine whose needs are the most urgent and what quantities of goods ought to be produced. These great disputes must result in an eventual allocation of resources that depends largely on how much one can influence the system by leveraging connections or by exaggerating their own needs to gain more out of the system[27].

From a moral standpoint, there can be a case made that that which is vital for people in society is intrinsically more valuable than that which is not vital for any given person. But this distinction is only practised to the absolute by very few people and holds no economic weight. People value their own well-being over the needs of others and we cannot universally condemn this as a negative thing. The only way that it is possible to have an economy without profit and have it function is either by using some form of market organization in the form of market socialism or mutual aid or by central planning. Expecting people to just be nice and share is not actionable to any extent and is not something that any person

---

[27] This can, to a large extent, be fixed when a society has incredibly high trust. However, the leftist anti-civilizational morality that the anarchists preach makes this an impossibility.

thinks ought to happen in reality as we can see by the lack of demonstrated preferences for the lifestyle[28].

Then there is the alternative where instead of systems of centralized production or production for profit, there is a system of mutual aid. This means that people will share their resources in a decentralized manner in such a way that each person supports each other person, but not that they get more out of the system than they put in. This mutual aid would not function by means of exchanging money in the form of subjective value but by exchanging goods for an equivalent amount of labour value[29] that was put into those goods. Thus creating a society where everyone gets exactly what they laboured for and nothing more than that amount. Since everyone gets precisely the amount that is represented in their commitment to labour, the economy avoids the problems with the previous approach without creating a system that produces profit for capitalists. Other than different forms of market socialism, this is certainly the best possible socialist replacement for capitalism and is extremely hard to dispute in any way that does not simply condemn it as utopian without providing an argument.

However, even though this ideology does not possess any personal pitfalls and it avoids a lot of problems due to the fact that

---

28

From this, we can elaborate that socialists expect to profit from socialism, which is why they are not currently redistributing their own resources. If socialists were arguing for socialism in good faith, they would actively be doing everything to help workers suffering under capitalism.

29

Labour value usually refers to the average social labour-time put into producing a certain good.

it often proposes an establishment of a bank that can loan resources at no interest other than what is required for upkeep, it still has one crucial issue. That is that when goods are exchanged for the amount of labour they possess and not by the amount of value they have in the eyes of each individual, there will always be an inefficient allocation of resources. Even though supply and demand can take effect in the broadest sense, all calculation is disrupted by the fact that the supply and demand in this economy lack a way in which to receive economic signals. There is no way to tell if people want more or less of some good other than how much labour they are willing to invest into it for the exchange of an item of the same value of labour. This can also be represented in labour certificates that represent the labour they have expended in the production of their own goods. This means that the price system will be disturbed which will not cause surpluses or shortages but rather cause people to allocate resources inefficiently.

On a free capitalist market, when people buy a certain amount of a cheaper commodity and forgo more expensive commodities, it causes there to be a need to reduce the prices of those commodities. When the prices of commodities are created due to the labour involved, there is scarcely any need for people to move into new industries or industries that lack supply. The only incentive there is to leave industries is that production that people no longer want and thus gets excluded from this system of mutual aid. Furthermore, people are incentivized to move into more labour intensive industries to be able to profit more instead of moving into industries that are more automated, this will lead to a general misallocation of resources[30].

---

[30] As this chapter is heavy on theory and I am not an expert on anarchism, it could be that I misrepresented a position, use discretion if necessary.

VI – Bosses

The anarchist philosophy is fundamentally opposed to any and all command structures and one of their romanticised criticisms of capitalism is that it inherently has bosses, which means having systems of economic command. Anarchist opposition to bosses is based on many reasons, however, this is mainly a moral issue of independence so I have to first demonstrate how one can feasibly function in capitalism without a boss and how it is not necessary to utilize bosses. Even though economically it should be undeniable that a system of bosses will create a more efficient allocation of resources, on a personal level that doesn't always mean much.

First, if there is pure capitalism in the post-industrial era, there is no need for any person to work in a traditional work environment. The eternal example is that anyone is free to return to subsistence farming or use the market to go beyond subsistence farming yet still run an independent farm to feed themselves. This is a drastic reduction to the quality of life when one has grown accustomed to technology and luxury, but if independence is such an important aspect of life, there is nothing stopping anyone from forming a homestead other than a monopoly on land by the government. And no capitalist should have the power to buy empty unused land, as no one owns the empty and unused land. Property rights should come from actionable claims and not just simple declarations and acts of throwing money at the state. This means that the problem here is only that the state does not allow people to claim empty land to form a homestead on and not that the system of capitalism is oppressive.

Another way to avoid bosses is to start a co-operative enterprise with other workers where decisions are made democratically. By doing this it is possible to avoid bosses and still integrate yourself into the capitalist system and enjoy the luxuries of the capitalist system. Nothing forbids this sort of socialistic organizing as no capitalist, in a pure capitalist economic order, has the power to remove market competition if they do not agree with the structure it takes. The only problem with this is that the state again incentivizes corporations and not independent enterprises[31] so the problem again lies in the state. Anyone can also start a completely solitary enterprise where they are in complete control of all decisions and where they buy all of their own wares and sell the products that they themselves create. There is nothing stopping any person from doing this other than not having anything valuable to offer[32]. This requires taking investments or loans, however, these too may be organized socialistically in the form of mutual aid systems. This can't be an inherent complaint as there is no systematic lack of access to capital when individuals can provide their labour by alternative means in the market in any way they choose to.

31

      Even with this being true, there are still many cases of workplaces that actively practice worker democracy.

32

      E-commerce and other digital trading have made it feasible to even earn a good income by working a solitary enterprise.

Of course, all these paths are much harder than the conventional path of working for a boss and earning a wage, but if independence is a moral issue, then these all should be valid options and something that any proper anarchist is willing to do. If it goes against human decency to be beholden to the wishes of some boss, you can assert your decency, but by doing so you will have to contribute incredible amounts of resources and labour, far more than the conveniences of conventional capitalism would require you to. If you are not ready to work hard for independence, then you cannot claim that it is an issue that transcends economics, personal desires or politics. And this problem is always pervasive to some extent in anarchist societies because there are no bosses to take some of this workload and responsibility onto themselves. The price for independence is spread across the entirety of society.

The only counter-argument anarchists have is that the capitalists systematically collaborate in order to restrict access to capital so they are to blame that the anarchic society cannot take shape. If only the anarchists had some starting capital which they could obtain via a revolution they would quickly achieve their utopia where workers control their own destiny. But this is absurd if you're not willing to start from the beginning and work your alternative society up from the ground, how would you be ready for a revolution. It may be that your life is worth less to you than a lot of effort, but revolutions require much more sacrifice than just peaceful co-operation and building a society where workers can be independent. Or the workers can use the resources that they have available from capitalistic production and wealthy sympathizers[33] can donate their estate and join the ranks of anarchistic workers and thus create an anarchist society without the need to overthrow capitalism. The assumption that all changes need to be sweeping revolutions is idealistic and plainly absurd.

The other objection to this is that having a boss goes contrary to human rights, so the issue is not one that can be solved peacefully but the entire working class needs to be liberated for there to be justice in the world. Liberate the working class if you so desire, but do this by outcompeting the capitalists who violate human rights and allow workers the choice to self-determine. There is no need to force workers to be anarchists if they do not want anarchy, give workers the option for anarchy and then see if these miserable people whose human rights are violated will become liberated. You can spread as much propaganda as you want to, advertise the anarchist way of life to your heart's content, and do everything in your power to make workers realize that they are oppressed, and if you are right then the workers will join your society instead of the capitalistic one. If workers do not want freedom from bosses, then why should you force it upon them[34]?

And this takes me to the main point, all the problems that are raised with individuals starting to form anarchistic societies

---

[33] Socialism has a history of being bourgeoisie, so this is not unfeasible.

[34] It is a popular notion that freedom bears no cost, but in every real-world scenario, freedom inherently includes the requirement to give up subsidy. Being unfree usually means having some social function taken care of as a fundamental condition of life.

become apparent in anarchistic societies. Without a capitalistic class, the capital has to come from individual people and councils and there will be a systematic deficit of capital as people do not want to work more than they have to in order to contribute to keeping the society afloat. Establishing new enterprises when the risk is socialized and the cost is paid fully by people who do not especially benefit from those enterprises is very complicated. This freedom makes life a lot harder for a lot of people who have to devote themselves to worrying about the social well-being instead of just being able to worry about themselves. Even though social consciousness might be some sort of ideal, this is not the life most people would prefer if given a choice to live as they please.

And this extends down to individual enterprises in an anarchistic society when the system of production produces for need and the mechanisms of production are decided democratically, each person needs to concern himself with the social system instead of contributing to himself. This causes headache a lot of people would rather avoid and delegate to someone else, this can be solved by giving councils any sort of authority, but this would go against anarchism. If the councils do not exercise any real authority and if social needs are decided democratically with only using the councils as guidance, each worker has to take onto himself the role that was otherwise completely handled by the boss.

This democratic and perverted self-determination might be desirable for some, but it includes taking care of a lot of tasks on an individual level that the boss would have had to take care of otherwise. Since these tasks are democratic, each person has to take the role a full-time boss would have taken otherwise. Each person then has to fundamentally work multiple jobs, rendering the anarchist promise of less work absolutely empty. The only way to solve this is to give councils authority or to embrace left-wing market anarchism. But both of these solutions also have problems. With the councils you only shift the nature of bosses, instead of working for profit, the bosses work for the supposed social good, which is a much worse motivator and has always ended in causing an exercise of power that ultimately leads to personal profit. With the market anarchist structure, the workers would still be the shareholders and have to make business decisions even though they can delegate the managerial duties, they can't be divorced from the role that was previously filled by the boss.

In a capitalistic system, any concrete worker has no need to concern themselves with managerial duties unless those have been individually delegated to that worker. The workers don't need to make business decisions and the business decisions are made by people more capable of making those decisions than the workers are. It may be an aesthetically pleasing system where the workers organize completely on their own, but it is a fundamental fact that workers can't have the same sort of business experience dedicated capitalists do. This must by necessity cause systemic inefficiency when it comes to organizing the economy. This is not to deride workers, capitalists would probably be similar failures if they would have to return to labour, this is just the result of specialization into different roles ensuring an order in which people can focus on what they are good at.

Another problem anarchists have with bosses is that they don't think any person should be robbed of their independence and that each person has the fundamental right to self-determine in their personal and economic life. This is one of the core philosophies of anarchism, they want to have radical independence and as such think that everyone else wants to have the same degree of independence. But this is not how humans operate. The vast majority of people prefer to be integrated into hierarchical control systems so they can fill their own social role without having to worry about others and being able to only focus on themselves. In this manner hierarchies create personal independence, they divorce people from roles that they have no need to fulfil. Most people prefer having bosses telling them what to do so they themselves don't have to decide what has to be done, for the majority this is normal and desirable and not in any way a negative outcome of the capitalistic system.

And as a final thing, there is the assumption that under capitalism each worker is just subject to the whims of their boss and that the boss is in control of the life of the worker. This ignores the fact that when there are healthy economies this is not the case as there are plenty of jobs available, this is only a problem when the economy is in a dysfunctional state for some reason or another. There can be a debate whether this is indigenous or exogenous, but capitalism, when it has been implemented in a way that is pure and proper, allows for people to find new jobs and to put their efforts into some other place. Workers are not beholden to what is demanded of them as long as they are allowed to choose whether or not they work in a certain enterprise. When capitalists are allowed to freely create capital, workers are allowed to freely quit their jobs as they are not bound to their boss.

Insula Qui

Progressive Critiques

I – Inequality

One of the common arguments progressives love to make against capitalism is how it makes people unequal and thus is a negative part of any society. This is usually followed up with proposing a welfare state to eliminate a degree of this inequality and to make people more equal and the society more egalitarian. This may seem like a common-sense criticism, it is hard to justify the existence of extremely wealthy people having as much money as they do while the poorest in society are starving. However, this is not the logic we use whenever anything else in society is unequal. We don't blame muscular men for creating inequality when it comes to being in shape or sociable lady-killers for making society more unequal for those men who can't talk to women. Why is wealth inequality such a special case?

First, I need to mention that capitalism only creates extreme inequality in two cases. The first case is whenever there is a state involved in capitalism, there will be people who want to buy access to that state and who want to use that state for their own personal gain. Investing in state violence will often prove itself to be a very valuable strategy. Since usually only rich people and populist coalitions of poor people can assemble the money to actually buy favours from the state, there will tend to be an increase in the wealth of the rich in society. This is simply because the persons within the state are as selfish and as greedy as everyone else, functionaries are motivated by their own desires and not some abstract common good. If someone can offer politicians and bureaucrats enough money so that they can rationalize violating some abstract principles, they will violate these abstract principles. The simple fact of being appointed into the state bureaucracy or receiving a certain amount of votes does not make anyone into a good person.

When the rich are able to purchase access to the state they can do two things, first they can change the institutional incentives within the system to benefit them and allow for greater wealth accumulation. We see this happening very often with big corporations wanting additional regulatory burdens for their own personal gain. Erecting barriers to entry for industries is much more profitable for the big companies as the small companies will not be able to burden the cost. The second thing that a capitalist can do when he has access to the state is the direct redistribution of wealth, he can ask for subsidies, monopoly rights and every other redistributive measure which would serve to enrich the capitalist. All this gain is parasitic and coercively appropriated from the other people in the economy. The poor can do this too, but to a much more limited extent, they can only get benefits insofar as they need to be appeased. When the class conflict between the different groups within a state escalates, the government is well served by providing the poor with some degree of benefits to simply make them stop being angry. This ensures compliance and an elevated role of the state in the economy, causing the poor to constantly increase the status and power of the state.

Thus whenever there is a combination of the state and of capitalism, there must be increasing inequality due to institutional benefits for the rich. But there is another way in which there can be extreme inequality, that is there can be extreme differences in the quality and the quantity of output. This is how people like Jeff Bezos and John D. Rockefeller manage to obtain as much money as they do. No one can deny that the incredible amounts by which Bezos has brought down transaction costs and how much Rockefeller was able to reduce the price of oil and increase the efficiency of oil production[35] are socially worth the fortunes these men made in their lifetimes. Their ingenuity served and still serves as the cornerstone of industry in their era and the way in which these people were able to manage their capital extremely efficiently proved to be an immense social benefit. Amazon is a vital service when it comes to e-commerce and Standard Oil served as the basis of most modern industrialism. These men only proportionally benefited from the wealth they created for the entirety of society.

It would be absurd to claim that people who are incredibly wealthy only due to providing such an immense service didn't earn the extreme amounts of wealth. The impact these sorts of people have is so rare and such an important aspect of the economy that they deserve to be rewarded to the extent they have been. This is true except for the case where a portion of their wealth is built up by using the state to their own advantage. And it is true that anyone else could have done the same things that these brilliant men did, but it is also true that no one else was as quick or as good at it. This

---

[35]

    Thomas DiLorenzo has written an excellent paper on this titled "The Myth of Predatory Pricing".

allowed these extremely rich capitalists to profit as much as they have profited in the first place. Furthermore, these are people who are gifted with both the abilities to be an entrepreneur and to continue their entrepreneurship while their company has grown immensely. The sort of brilliant minds who can do both are few and far between. Having people who can carry their vision even when their companies are already prosperous and large results in a constant spirit of innovation. This incredible innovation is only possible because these men are themselves gifted beyond ordinary people.

And this leads me to the next point, inequality is often the result of natural and unchangeable hierarchy within society, this is not to say that the wealthiest people are the best people, but rather that they are the best at producing wealth. When people are vital to the economy and increasingly important to others, they gain more profits as they provide better services. And hierarchy is a fact of nature, status and personal placement within society and the economy are vital to ensure a structured society. In this capacity, all egalitarianism must destroy society by erasing the fundamental connections between those within society. We can imagine an alternative world where the earnings of everyone would be completely random and thus the perceived hierarchy would be one where people who have excess resources are ones that are selected on the basis of no merit and no importance. If this is the case, then social classes would cease to exist in any meaningful way and would instead be replaced by groups of people who share no common virtue and who are all only defined by the amount of resources they own. If this were to happen, you could have both bums and geniuses relegated to a vague middle-class classification and experience a complete breakdown in society.

However, what you see in any free market society is that you have distinct social groups and a hierarchy which is relatively based on the merit of the people in lower and upper classes. It is not important whether this merit is personally or socially generated as it would be naive and absurd to expect equality when there is any individuality or liberty. The most that can feasibly be done is to strive for an elevation of the people who would otherwise be socially at risk[36]. This is defined by the economic roles these people occupy and economic hierarchy eliminates potential disorder. In the market economy, the role of the capitalist is to serve the consumer. If we placed a person who is not fit to cater to consumers into the role of having vast amounts of capital, that person will not become a fit capitalist.

People will retain their nature and their station in society no matter how much anyone can try to fix that. However, inasmuch as people retain their station in society, they also gravitate towards the most appropriate place in the hierarchy. A child born to a poor family may grow up to be incredibly wealthy and a child born to a wealthy family may group up to be incredibly poor. This is inherently dependent on the values of these people, their immutable biology, and the skills that they themselves accumulate.

---

[36] This does not imply any degree of state intervention, rather it can be just as well be a matter of private investment and voluntary contributions to the parts of society who are considered to be the most at risk.

All people have a chance to increase their productivity and change their economic role and thus change their place in the economic hierarchy, but this correlates to the good features of these people themselves and not some broad injustice.

In the capitalist economy, there develops a defined hierarchy on the basis of the comparative importance of different social roles. But this hierarchy does not judge value, even though there are many more janitors and they are thus less valuable than the aptest managers, without these janitors there could never be managers. Furthermore, roles such as priesthood and motherhood, while not being economically lucrative, are still socially valued outside the material economy. And even when a worker is interchangeable with most all other workers, they are vital to the economy at large. A manager has the important role of performing mundane economic operations in such a way that the firm and by extension society benefits, which places more responsibility onto the manager. This is because, in a system of pure capitalism, the only way to profit is to make others profit alongside you.

The capitalist is also interchangeable with other capitalists but serves the extremely important role of providing capital to the efforts that are worth taking. There are finer class distinctions and there are complex economic operations, but fundamentally what we see in capitalism is some variation of these three class activities. Furthermore, most people partake in elements of all of these to some extent, if you keep your money in a bank which earns interest, you are in essence a capitalist. If you do manual labour at any point in your life, you are a worker. And if you ever exert any sort of control over your personal economic actions, you serve as a manager of sorts. The distinctions become entirely dependent on how well-equipped any person is to fill the role of the capitalist, worker or manager.

All of these virtues are vital for the organization of society. All of these classes are vital to ensure that any society could function and are economically vital for any sort of organization. All of the virtues of all of these social classes can be corrupted, but if capitalism is combined with a proper sense of morality. There exists an unequal allocation of social roles which creates a solid and orderly hierarchy with people who can fill the roles needed in society. And you need people focusing on every level of centralization and decentralization and you need people with different visions, and this is what you see with all of these class identifications. Every part of economic life becomes delegated to a certain class and as such the virtue in these roles can be cultivated.

You could still conceptually be opposed to the inequality in capitalism and you could still think that this is a bad part of the capitalistic system. But this ignores the fact that humans are drawn to hierarchies by their own natures and that people, when faced with chaos from a lack of hierarchy, tend to not have properly delegated social roles. This, in turn, lowers the quality of life for each person. When a person has no role to play within society, then that person also will to a large extent lack meaning in his activities and act according to nothing other than momentary whims. Furthermore, this clear and defined social hierarchy ensures that the people who are unfit for the position they hold currently always have something concrete to set as their goal and capitalism allows people to ascend hierarchies by their own virtue. And this is the distinction between a capitalist class and a caste when someone is a part of the caste system, there is no upward mobility. It has always been the case that under capitalism, the greatest can move up and no person is stuck in any caste. This does not mean that every person can be economically mobile, but rather every person who should have economic mobility will have it.

There's one last point to address, even if in the perfect interpretation of economic theory, inequality would not be negative there's still the problem of intergenerational hierarchy. This means that people can be in an economic position they should not be in because their parents lacked the resources to open the opportunities that are needed for advancement. This is a valid criticism if you adopt the wrong perspective, you can't say that the child will have an invalid position in the hierarchy as the child is not the relevant actor. What instead happens is that the parents who were able to secure for themselves the position in the social hierarchy, are also able to provide for their children in accordance with what they have earned. Exceptionally dull or brilliant children who are unfit for the economic role that their parents handed down will more often than not move upwards or downwards in the capitalist class system.

II – Poverty

One of the most often heard objections to capitalism is to point out the number of people who die from poverty or various other causes related to not having access to resources that would otherwise allow them to live. Another argument can be that just the existence of people who live in general misery, and not in the capitalist prosperity we are accustomed to, proves the evil of capitalism. The ultimate conclusion of this is to blame the greedy capitalists and call upon the wise, enlightened state to end poverty. This is obviously done by taking the money that capitalists hoard and distributing it among the population to increase their quality of life. If the population gained access to this wealth, they would not have to deal with poverty. Furthermore, since the capitalists have immense amounts of wealth, they would not miss the portion of their money that is taken from them in any way. This is at least when compared to the general social utility redistribution would bring. And society itself would be in a generally better place with a more seemingly just allocation of resources.

We can philosophically base the abolition of poverty around the notion that all humans deserve the basic necessities of life. The problem here is the fact that someone needs to have money taken from them, in effect some people need to be punished for having the gall to have money in order for there to be any redistribution. Why is it necessary to take from the people who are able to provide for themselves and give to the people who are not? And where does anyone get the right to take money from various people so that they can give that money to other people? It seems as if the only truly ethical way to ease poverty is through voluntary aid, but supposedly a person's right to life trumps the right to property. And we may say that it is a human right to have these necessities as they facilitate life. But it still seems absurd to put this right above the right to keep the property that you have earned fairly by nonviolent means. Should it not be one of the greatest human rights to not be looted whenever someone needs something? Weakening the right to property will always eventually weaken society as a whole as that society will never be secure in its property.

There are three arguments to combat this. First, no one earns money in a vacuum and all people require a robust capital structure and a workforce to have money at all. Second, there is an inherent obligation to the society where one lives in and the state has a right to use that obligation to make people pay for the privilege of living in the society where they reside. Third, that the state is the only thing that can provide property rights and we all need the state to do any business. If the state demands that we give it any amount of money, then we need to do so as our wealth is only possible because of the state. If the state decides to redistribute wealth, it is only the prerogative of the state.

The answer to the first objection is fairly simple, we may say that the people who get rich only get rich because they can employ other people. Since they need employees, they owe some degree of obligation to those who work for them and the society the capitalist operates in. But this still does not justify the state being able to take as much money as they want, even if there is an inherent obligation to society, it does not mean that the state ought to enforce it. The institutions of community and church are much better fit to distribute wealth to those in need. Furthermore, the capitalist has already paid for the wages of the workers and the resources he used in doing his business, he has also sold his products in productive exchange. There is no further need to demand that the state imposes any penalties on his wealth. If the workers want higher wages or more benefits, that's a matter to be discussed between the worker and the employer and not the state and the employer. This issue is not one that is supposed to be addressed by the state.

The second concept relies on a fictional social contract that embodies the society and binds everyone to certain duties for the furtherment of the society. The easiest way to defeat this argument is simply to point out that no one in any society consents to this social contract without being threatened by force and as such, they are not in any moral way required to follow this social contract. There is the absurd notion that somehow the wealthy have not already given enough back to society. This is based on a complete misconception of where wealth comes from, it's not like the people who get wealthy do so by doing nothing, but rather they sell products or offer services and get money in return. The giving back was done when they provided the service or the product and there is nothing more to the interaction than the transaction that has already taken place, there is no obligation after getting wealthy than what it took to get wealthy in the first place, this is unless the wealth was obtained by unscrupulous means.

The final argument is that the state holds the society together so everyone has an obligation to the state. There could be no wealth without the state being involved in the first place. Since it is necessary that the state is involved, it can then demand a portion of the profits in society to be allocated to the uses of the state. One of these uses is providing for those who are needy and who require assistance. The social role of the state is not only to incentivize production but also to form a safety net and protect the population against themselves.

But the state itself has never done actual work at all! The supposed social cohesion is achieved by the police, the military, and other individuals. This is at least when the people who the state pays are working in the interests of the people and within the bounds of the social role that they themselves are responsible for. These are not the actions of the state but the individuals employed by the state, and these individuals could just as well be employed by communities in the same way they would be in any other industry. All services could be directly funded by the people in communities themselves pooling their money without taxation. However, the state has taken upon itself the role of providing services, which is not a testament to the importance of the state but rather the power of the state.

This means nothing other than that the state has obtained a monopoly and freed itself completely from accountability. It should serve as a testament to the immorality of the state and not that the state is a great benefactor without which we could not be able to live our lives. We can say that law and order are great necessities and that defence is similarly vital. But the importance of vital services does not mean that any centralized agency can take upon itself law, order and defence and be a completely moral barrier against chaos.

Then there is the other side of the issue, the question whether the alleviation of poverty can really be considered a right or if people in poverty are impoverished because of themselves or because of society. There is a case to be made that trying to eliminate poverty through the state may only create more poverty. Welfarism has become a humanitarian idol and implying that we should not help the poor and the sick via the state is tantamount to saying that we wish babies to die. If we dare to oppose this system then the opposition can only be due to an anti-social line of thinking as people will die if they are not guaranteed life and that removing the existing protections will cost lives.

But this assumes that each person inherently deserves all that they need to live and that there is no individual responsibility to provide for yourself. This is absurd to everyone who has ever seen the reality of the world outside of a classroom. The notion that the lack of an ability to provide for yourself entitles you to some special benefits should be an extremely immoral statement. It is made even worse by the relative ease with which people can provide for themselves in the modern economy. It should not be something logical or rational or polite, but rather it ought to be thoroughly repulsive to imply that everyone should be responsible for the well-being of the people who are unable to actually take care of themselves. To say that people do not have to earn compassion to be taken care of only results in anti-social behaviour.

Firstly, welfarism promotes being unable to provide for your own self as the people who can't provide anything receive special benefits. Because people who are useless receive benefits unconditionally, there will be an increased amount of people who want to receive benefits and who will opt to use the generous systems in place to sustain themselves while they do nothing as this is a possible replacement for productive labour and living an actual life, this is a very dangerous trap. Furthermore, unconditional and impersonal welfare prevents people from doing something productive as that would result in them losing money. If they lost the help of aid programs, then they would be harming their finances for no good reason and they have to remain useless if they wish to keep getting aid. This so-called help will always increase the amount of uselessness in any society and this is by design as there is no need for the state to get rid of the people who are acting as parasites upon the system. The more people are dependent on the state, the more people will be invested in the state and will uphold the state.

Secondly, each person should have a responsibility for his own affairs before worrying about the affairs of others. Many of the people who are taxed by the state to provide for the people who can't work are people who are themselves heavily in need of money. If their money is taxed, they are in turn unable to care for themselves as they are forced to provide for the people who can't provide for themselves at all. It's not as if a simple level of wealth can even determine whether or not a person is in a good position when it comes to finances, some people have necessities such as children and medical bills that are not covered by the state and they need to take care of. The only other solution to this is to nationalize all services that could be necessary for life. If we are not willing to nationalize almost everything that serves as a necessity, we cannot ever assume that taxing people based on income will result in a just allocation of wealth. The most basic part of society should always be to make sure that you yourself can live before taking care of others.

And finally, we need to consider that the state taking care of everyone has devastating effects on the people who are supposed to take care of each other as they no longer have any economic reason to do so. Without the state, you need to rely on your family and community as there are always unexpected troubles that can cause great problems in personal lives. Without the need for personal supportive institutions as the state covers the finances of everyone, we can only expect there to be less family and less community. If we want to incentivize the institutions that are vital for the development of a healthy society, we can not let the state usurp their role. The support provided by the state is an anti-social safety net.

The state additionally takes away the moral well-being that comes with charity and largely reduces the importance of social bonds formed by charity. If the state is not in control of welfare, private individuals can enjoy giving to others and helping their fellow man in need. However, if the state usurps welfare, there is no possibility to gain personal enjoyment out of the help that is done with your money by the government. Moreover, it is not as if all money taxed is spent in aiding the community, a significant portion of total taxed revenue goes towards purposes where there is a significant degree of disagreement and purposes that are objectionable to some. If this is the case, what the state may consider aid may be an immoral use of resources. As such the state replaces what could have been the joy of giving with the dread of taking and then the added uncertainty about whether or not the money that was taken will be used in a decent and moral manner.

III – Conservationism

An often heard criticism of capitalism is that limited resources will soon be exhausted or rampant industrialism will pollute the environment beyond saving. Whenever there is a possibility for blaming capitalism as going against ecology, there are always people who will do so. This is supposedly backed by the undeniable fact that capitalist industries constantly go against nature by design and capitalism in itself encourages pollution. Some treat this as definitive proof that in order to remove the possibility of ecosystems breaking down, we need to remove capitalism. Libertarians are sometimes quick to say that this doesn't matter and the market will decide what's best for humans, and if this means pollution, then let it be pollution, they do this while ignoring all the disastrous long-run effects of ruining the environment.

The most vital part of conservationism within a free market is the marketization of currently non-market resources. There is a good reason why the interests of capitalist industries always seem to trump the interests of nature, this is because nature is not yet a capitalist industry. There is no reason why nature should not conform to economic law, marketization is the best possible way to maintain and improve nature for nature to be sustainable in the long term and yet consistently produce value even in the short term. If nature as a good that people want to consume is held by private hands and the goods provided by nature are distributed on the basis of free pricing, then there is no way that nature will be used in a way that is improper or unprofitable. If the goods provided by nature and nature itself become privately owned, there are tremendous incentives for protecting nature.

This is because whenever capitalists expect to profit from their property or capital, they will defend their property and capital. When all nature is explicitly or implicitly managed and owned by the state, there can be no such claim that the state will defend it. After all, the state can only sell temporary access to nature and the amount of access sold will always correspond to the incentives of the state and not of the public. Thus access to nature is bought by capitalists and the state is beholden to the wishes of those who pollute and consume. However, pollution and reckless use would make no sense when it is a matter of your own property. The state will always let the interests of the capital go against the interests of the public as the state is selling access to its land to the capitalists and not to the public. The only way to balance the profit motive with public interest is to allow full private ownership over nature. In a pure market environment, the only way to profit is to cater to the interests of the public.

But this may seem befuddling, it subverts all expectations one may have, it raises more questions than it answers, but those questions too have answers. The first objection is that there simply wouldn't be enough money for the purpose of preserving nature in a pristine state. But this is nonsensical, in reality, we see millions of people using nature for the sake of an aesthetic benefit. These millions would be very willing to pay to have access to pure nature even if it requires fees[37]. There is also tremendous amounts of money allocated to environmentalists and scientific purposes that require keeping land untainted. This logically also implies a market for conserving the land used for environmental or scientific purposes. Industrial capitalists are not the only people able to buy land, scientists and environmentalists could also buy the right to own land. With those rights, they could cultivate that land for their own purposes, whether those are providing a habitat for a threatened species or observing some plant in its natural condition.

Secondly, there is the problem that the ownership of nature simply seems wrong, private people shouldn't own what seems to currently belong to the public. Isn't the use and enjoyment of nature something that ought to belong to everyone? This is a valid perspective, but it also implies that pollution is a similarly legitimate use of nature. If establishing defined property rights goes against what unused land should be, then establishing property rights against pollution is also wrong. If natural land really should belong to everyone, why shouldn't it also belong to the polluters so that they can pollute it? The only way to get past this contradiction is to establish well-defined property rights, the owners of which can decide how the land will be used. If the government already claims property for itself and uses taxes to maintain it, it is no different than making nature exclusive for the

---

[37] This is not to say that fees will necessarily be charged, it is possible that the owners of a forest will instead try to use it as marketing to sell hunting or recreational supplies.

companies that privatize nature and charge fees for the use of that nature.

And the fees will be small, the costs of maintaining land for aesthetic enjoyment are minimal, provided that property rights are respected more often than not. The value of pure land is not a matter of resources or urban development, so the land is cheap. No one can predict the specific price of land set aside for aesthetic enjoyment, but, unless there is a giant demand, the fees charged will tend to be low. There are certainly areas which would require higher fees to access, but these are the greatest landmarks of a nation. This to the conservationist should be an additional benefit, as the greatest landmarks would remain relatively less spoiled from human use. Furthermore, the costs still couldn't be that high as there is still a need for people to come visit and pay the fees to see landmarks if the owners are to make a profit. The fees would have to be affordable enough that normal people can have the ability to experience the great landmarks[38].

And I would also like to make clear that this privately owned land doesn't need to be held by for-profit businesses. If environmentalist groups wanted to conserve some great swaths of land, they would be as within their rights to do so as anyone else, even if they forsook making a profit. This means that any and all fears about the greedy capitalists exploiting and making all land useless commodities are not based in reality. The marketization of land would mean that any group could spend their money on the

---

38

    And as mentioned before, fees can be supplanted by using landmarks to sell memorabilia.

market, the great amounts of resources that currently go into lobbying the government could instead be spent on accumulating various scenic land which can then be preserved and used only for those purposes that the conservationists deem fit.

Finally, the only reason why capitalists are able to pollute in such massive amounts as they do now is due to legislation. Capitalists and the state are not held responsible for their own pollution and the negative effects which pollution has. More likely than not, in a market-based law system, polluters would be held accountable for the harm they caused to everyone affected by their pollution. In this form, the damages caused to the body and material property of those affected by pollution must be reparated and the pollution must be ceased. This is unless the companies that want to pollute are able to buy the rights to pollute from the people who their pollution affects. This would especially help poor people as there is certainly bound to be some degree of pollution and the polluters having to pay for their pollution would greatly decrease the cost of living. Of course, this couldn't be deadly or extremely harmful, as in that case there wouldn't be enough people who would burden the cost of pollution. But when the alternative is homelessness or a much lesser quality home, it may serve as a great way to help the poor find housing. In a way, you would be using pollution to subsidize low-class housing, which is almost equivalent to the carbon tax schemes some environmentalists strongly favour.

IV – Democracy

The most absurd argument against capitalism or other voluntary systems of organization is that they are undemocratic and should be more subject to whatever is supposedly some higher will of the people. This democratic will somehow supersedes any individual relations people may have in business. If capitalism is not subject to this higher democracy, it must be completely worthless as a system since it goes against what the people themselves want. If capitalism is not democratic, the capitalists can obviously disregard what is good for actual people and instead exploit and domineer over society, only restricted by how much money they have. As we do not want to be domineered over, it would be undesirable to have capitalists excluded from democracy. The logic leads to a rejection of pure capitalism on the grounds that it can never be truly democratic and the people as a whole do not possess the power. Capitalism without democracy is equivalent to feudalism, with the simple change from manorialism to plutocracy.

However, this approach makes assumptions that are wildly ungrounded in any form of reality and ignores how capitalists function within society. The first and most grievous fault in this logic is that capitalists are always bound to the popular will, albeit in a form distinct from democracy. If capitalists put their resources into production for which there is no demand, then there could fundamentally not be any profit for the capitalists. If any capitalist even made a product that is slightly less desirable than another product, he will be completely outcompeted by the superior one.

This is not reflected in reality as the values of people differ and all capitalists frivolous enough to produce unwanted goods are not in positions of economic prominence. But this still warrants an example, we can imagine going to the store and finding a toothbrush completely made according to antique designs with natural bristles. Even though it is a novelty product, there is no way in which it can be sold when the alternative is a comfortable and modern toothbrush. And this is why we see continuous innovation in all capitalist industries.

This means that capitalists are strictly bound to the desires of their consumers and can never do anything if it goes against what the consumers demonstrably prefer. There is no way in which capitalists are able to profit if they do not strictly follow the desires of those who buy the products produced by the capitalists and there is no way in which capitalists can maintain their enterprise without continuous profit and constant success. The capitalists may do some immoral things besides their role in a market society and this will not necessarily affect their sales proportionally, but when it comes to market transactions capitalists must constantly follow what the people want. This capacity from immorality is not exclusive to capitalists, anyone can engage in violence and coercion.

Furthermore, politicians and state officials have no actual reason to follow what the people want them to do. There is no practical reason derived from self-interest which implies that a politician should do what the people want him to do. This is true unless the politician would face such a significant amount of backlash as to not get re-elected. The only motivation for a politician to ever do anything that the people want him to do is when that politician is under significant pressure. But this usually isn't the case with politicians, as there is very limited contact between ordinary people and the workings of the state. With politics, we can only cross our fingers and hope that everything turns out well. When it comes to market transactions, each person is subject to the consequences of their mistakes as when someone makes a bad decision on the market, they will lose their own money without getting adequate compensation in return. If a capitalist tries to produce something for which there is no demand, they will be out of their own money and have to themselves internalize the social loss. In this sense, markets could be even more democratic than the state ever is, when someone makes a mistake on the market, they will be pressured to correct that mistake.

There is also the complaint that democracy in itself is a hallowed system and anything that challenges democracy must be something negative. This too is grounded in nothing other than delusion. To say that there is anything special about casting votes to select leaders is similarly absurd. The fact that each person gets to vote does not imply anything other than that decisions are made by a given majority. There is nothing that fundamentally distinguishes democracy from other systems of politics other than current fashion considering democracy itself a human right. But this is only true as autocratic and oligarchic systems are seen to suppress human rights. Any preference for democracy is not because democracy is special, but rather democracy challenges the systems that are seen as having worse consequences. Democracy in itself is not a hallowed system, to imbue democracy with a form of spiritual mysticism goes contrary to reason. Democracy does not ensure that the state is controlled by the population, democracy only ensures that people are allowed a vote to choose from the options that the state allows. The majority in a vote is not necessarily what anyone wants, but only what is politically expedient at the point where a decision is made. There are no unique liberties that democracy provides, democracy can be as oppressive as any other system if the majority vote results in an oppressive regime.

And finally, there is the ever-present fear that without a popular government corporations will become the government and rule over people in a dictatorial fashion. If corporations are not subject to democracy, the seemingly obvious result is that they are able to engage in any unethical practice they desire. Whenever there is a free market, there is an area which is outside the scope of the state. The more capitalism there is, the less of society is subject to democracy as democracy functions only when making decisions for the entire society. Capitalism allows each person to choose what they sell and what they buy and this allows capitalists to be unrestrained in their control over society.

But this is only based on fantasy and not reflected in any real system. First of all, corporations are only in a privileged position because modern democratic states give them the ability to be entities separate from the people within the corporation. The reason why corporations can get away with what they get away with is that no person is responsible for any act committed by a corporation. And all businesses have to make money on the free market and trying to force a population to submit to the business will necessarily result in a loss of revenue. No one would let their capital be used by a business that is losing them money.

Even if ethical concerns were not problems for a business, having a near-guaranteed negative return on investment is not an appealing proposition. However, corporations still are able to use the existing governmental structures and simply pay comparatively small sums of money for lobbying and other influence based efforts. It is much easier for a corporation to control the popular government rather than to use violence by itself. The corruption present in the free market is always enabled by the state working in tandem with the businesses that it partners with. Businesses can only become corporations and use violence if violence is cheap enough, the only entity that benefits from a monopoly on violence that allows it to sell cheap violence at the cost of the society is the state.

V – Institutional Discrimination

A claim that emerged from a subsection of marxism that has recently become more mainstream is that capitalism as it currently stands is inherently racist. This idea has been around for very long, however, this notion of black socialism has seen growth with recent mass movements. This claim has two parts to it, first it correctly empirically analyzes that under the system of capitalism black people have less wealth than whites. Then from these premises, it concludes that the issue is with institutional racism. This is a very clever trick, it manages to play into both anti-racism and anti-capitalism. However, for the claim that capitalism is racist to be true, the following two statements have to be true.

First, capitalism cannot be based on personal merit, but rather has to be a system in which the institutional framework trumps individual initiative. This is a worthwhile thing to investigate and to handwave it away and simply state that capitalism by definition encourages individual initiative is a very close-minded approach. The conclusion also assumes that the only way a group can be less wealthy than another is if that group is being discriminated against. These two premises seem reasonable to a lot of people, especially those who have built their philosophy around both anti-racism and anti-capitalism, but this sentiment is not as convincing to anyone coming from different premises. Due to the clash of premises, the argument often revolves around miscommunication. Some even point out that the progressives are racist because they think blacks are not able to compete with whites provided that all are allowed to put forth their best effort on the free market. And truly if this were the case and if the utility of black people was almost negligible compared to the utility of white people, capitalism would be racist according to both definitions. In essence, the only way we can define capitalism as universally racist is if whites are superior in every regard.

However, that assertion is absurd as we can see that even in the supposedly institutionally racist system, black people often get hired to the detriment of whites and black people often make decent money. Thus we cannot assume that blacks are useless. To combat these claims we can only try to combat the premises. First, there is the thought-provoking question whether or not capitalism is really based on merit or whether meritocratic capitalism is just idealistic economic fiction. Both approaches have sound reasoning behind them, even though the proponents of either perspective will act as if the opposition fundamentally misunderstands capitalism. First, we have the socialist approach which characterizes capitalism as the institutional class domination by the capitalist class, or in this case, the white class. Since the capitalist or white class is dominant then it would be obvious that there can be no merit-based hierarchy in capitalism. A dominant class can always control the political economy in a manner that will benefit them. Furthermore, any socialistic system perceived to be truly meritocratic will never be allowed to take root, as it directly goes against the dominant class.

Due to this domination by the ruling class, it becomes fundamentally absurd to state that capitalism is based on merit.

This is further reinforced by the existence of inheritance as wealth being transferred intergenerationally is seemingly a sure way to showcase how capitalism doesn't favour merit but rather being a part of the dominant class. After all, a person can inherit a fortune without himself showing any merit. The counterargument to this can only be that there is no ruling class or that the existence of the ruling capitalist class creates an inherently uncapitalistic society. Whenever political or economic power is concentrated in one class of people, the argument can be made that there can be no capitalism. Since there can be no capitalism if the market is controlled by any elite group, there can be no such thing as institutional discrimination. In this manner, you will find individual initiative trumping all else.

But both sides are ignorant, the first is ignorant of the history of capitalism, the second is ignorant of the present state of capitalism. We can distinctly historically point to a time where capitalism was based on merit. After the former aristocracy had lost their economic power and before the 20th century created the modern economy, there was a period of capitalism which was based on merit and where the individual initiative was supreme. Most socialist critiques of capitalism come from this time period and most arguments against capitalism use historical critiques that were aimed at the supposedly destructive power of the free market. However, the modern economy has drastically changed the nature of capitalism. We can no longer say that individual merit has anything to do with success in the framework of the market. Capitalism, as it stands, is a hollow shell of its former self. This can be described as inevitable, but if we worship the current state of capitalism, we are trying to argue for what is essentially not the sort of capitalism that we ourselves want.

However, even though all socialist theory is not completely useless and can help with us analyzing how capitalism is as it stands, a large amount of the reason for why capitalism has reached the current state is the progressive movement of the early 20th century. It has been forgotten within the narrative of trust-busting that progressive businessmen were largely motivated by a promise of economic centralization. The conservative writers still delude themselves into thinking that capitalism is still how it used to be a century or more ago. We cannot ignore that we have currently reached a stage in capitalism where perpetual moves away from capitalism have created the system that socialists were predicting. This does not imply that socialism is correct, but only that socialists had a realistic view of the direction that capitalism was on. For this reason, appeals to the free market will fall on deaf ears.

We can't even point to past U.S. capitalism to demonstrate how capitalism is not racist as any historical era has usually been more racist than the current time. The closest we get is the fact that segregation had to be legally enforced, but this is in itself not proof as after segregation stopped being enforced, integration became the legal norm that businesses had to follow. We have not had an exercise in modern history where people were allowed to discriminate or not according to their own preference. Rather what we can gather from history is only that capitalism isn't necessarily a system where institutional frameworks are dominant over individual initiative. Although it is somewhat absurd to refer to the era in which there was segregation or in which slavery was not yet abolished in the United States to formulate an argument against the charge that capitalism is racist. A less absurd example is the Nordic states in the 19th and early 20th centuries, there was no slavery and a free market dominated by individual initiative. This proves that conceptually there can be meritocratic capitalism without racism.

Furthermore, we need to address the claim that poverty is caused by discrimination and not other reasons. If we simply refer to government statistics on poverty and welfare use, we cannot accurately say that this is due to institutional discrimination. Rather a far more likely explanation is that the pro-black and pro-poor welfare programs have been curtailing blacks and placing them in a system of government dependency. When people are paid to be poor, more people will choose to be poor. When the state wants to appease its black population, it is easy to ensure dependence on welfare as a solution to make the black population docile. If this is the case, it has been a giant conspiracy by the state and not the doing of the free market. In this way, black people get their welfare and the ruling regime gets popular support. The institutions which are purported as helping disadvantaged people may be creating groups who are not able to care for themselves and are intentionally disadvantaged[39]. And this makes sense when you make not working a viable career path, fewer people will work. It

---

39

may not even have racist intentions, but a large cause of white domination may be simply the fact that white people were not as prone to being in poverty when these programs were implemented.

And we can't ignore the problem of black adjustment to the capitalist economy due to centuries of governmental discrimination that effectively barred the entire black population from the free market. As there is a history of government enforced racism, we must conclude that the problem here is a historic lack of capitalism causing ills in the black community. This is largely irrelevant when discussing whether or not the modern economy helps or hurts black people. Furthermore, if we are to say that the state is an inherent part of the capitalist apparatus and criticizing the state is the same as criticizing capitalism, we also need to be completely intellectually honest. The state with it's selective anti-discrimination and affirmative action has been acting seemingly to create black domination. Furthermore, the people paying for state funded programs that black people use are overwhelmingly white. We cannot make the case that the state is racist and as such capitalism is racist without acknowledging that the state has been selectively creating a favoured class out of minorities.

We can honestly admit two things now that we have discussed the premises. First that the modern capitalist economy is not a free market and there are institutional frameworks within this system that trump individual initiative. Secondly, capitalism does not necessarily have to be built upon institutional unfairness to

---

It is established that feeding wild animals is a bad practice as they will get dependent on the feeding, there is no reason that this would not apply to any group of people.

function, the fact that it has been so in recent history and in the United States is just a historical accident. Third, even institutional benefits can cause adverse effects on a societal scale. Thus it is possible to conclude that institutional discrimination is not something that must be inherent in capitalism.

However, why is this more likely than the notion that blacks are systematically discriminated against? This question should be answered by the political state of any multiracial country. It is downright illegal or extremely taboo to speak ill of any non-whites in public and furthermore, we see how people who are not white benefit from the government on a strictly monetary scale more than white people do. The two institutions that may be then discriminatory are the executors of law and corporations within the economy. Considering that corporations mandate progressive diversity quotas we can safely assume that corporate discrimination is not an institutional issue, at least not against non-whites. The executors of the law may be racist and there is no conclusive proof either way, although racist judges and police officers cannot explain systematic poverty within black communities. This leads us almost inevitably to either an argument for white supremacy or an argument for incentives working against groups that can only be solved with more capitalism.

VI – Healthcare

One of the hallmarks of modern progressivism is the insistence upon universal or nationalized healthcare. There are two ways one can make the case for collectivizing healthcare, the first is the way that is no backed by reality and the second way is actually useful and a great economic debate to be had about competition. I will address the first before I get to the second one.

The first way to argue for universal healthcare is some variation for the following logic: healthcare is expensive, everyone needs healthcare, let's have everyone pay for healthcare. It seems simple enough but it misses every core concept necessary to understand the topic, it fails at every step it tries to take and falls flat logically. First, it does not address why healthcare is expensive or consider that there may be ways to make healthcare less expensive. It simply takes as a given that under a free market system healthcare will be expensive without any proper arguments for why this is necessarily the case. The only proof of the high market cost of healthcare is the comparison of relatively cheaper European systems with the more expensive American system. This ignores any other reason for why healthcare in America is as expensive as it is. It is necessary to consider that the fact that healthcare is extremely expensive may have something to do with what the government does with healthcare already.

And there are many things that could be done to make healthcare less expensive. Most countries have some form of a monopoly over the certification of healthcare professionals or giant healthcare lobbies. Removing these influences will cause there to be a lesser barrier to entry and will make healthcare more accessible without any drop in quality. This is not to say that the qualifications for healthcare will be less stringent, but rather that they will be provided in a manner which does not disqualify quality practices. It may still be said that we need centralized regulation for proper quality assurance, but this is incorrect as most industries already use decentralized controls for quality in addition to the state-mandated controls. And this does not even require an abolition of the laws regarding cleanliness and other quality, but rather simply not giving a monopolistic agency the power to license businesses. These are problems within individual transactions that are best solved by courts and in arbitration.

We could also reduce the amount of union control over government when it relates to healthcare and let nurses and doctors fulfil roles that currently only specialists can perform. Simple procedures do not need multiple doctors that are all certified specialists and can be handled by capable doctors on their own. This would enable medical practice without having to use additional people who only large hospitals can afford to have on staff. This would be a great boon to smaller practices and would make it possible for there to be any actual competition.

And the final important thing is to eliminate the necessity for people to get their healthcare through their employer due to tax incentives and allow for equal treatment of health insurance through employers and in personal purchases. Having people personally choose their prices and plans must necessarily result in a heightened awareness of the available options and thus an actual market in healthcare. This is very centric to America but a lot of the problems with expensive healthcare do affect America the most. This means that we need to consider America as the main subject when we talk about healthcare. If these three things are done, healthcare as a whole would be much cheaper than it is right now by itself and there is no need to do anything further. A large part of the solution must be to remove institutional issues which are actively increasing the cost of healthcare without increasing the quality of healthcare. If we want to make unions, pharmaceutical companies and lobbyists better off, we can safely neglect this argument and still desire collectivized healthcare. If our goal is to help the people who suffer from the high costs of healthcare, it is vital to make it possible to lower the cost of healthcare.

But there can still be doubts that personal control over finances and competition cannot reduce the price of healthcare sufficiently to make a difference. But to combat this we can simply bring the issue down to a personal level. If an employer is offered three choices for health insurance, all of these are bound by one giant union of lobbyists and pharmaceutical companies in the form of the American Medical Association, the employer will make the decision that can bring him the most revenue. As the employer gets unique tax breaks and the cost is diffused across a large amount of people, there will be an increase in the prices of all healthcare services. If there is no such conglomeration of medical professionals with sway over government and if each person themselves has to pay for their own healthcare, the only way to increase revenues is to be better than the market competitors. The only way to do this is to either lower costs or increase quality, which will ensure that each person can get the best quality healthcare at the lowest cost.

The second assumption of the first argument is also faulty, it is true everyone has the potential to require healthcare, but that does not mean that everyone actively requires healthcare or that everyone is at the same risk of requiring healthcare. If we assume that everyone requires healthcare we will punish those who take care of their health and reward those who do not. If we want to maintain healthy populations[40] then we should not enable a mode of behaviour that is detrimental to individual health. And if unhealthy people are grouped with healthy people, there is another problem as the prices of healthcare will need to go up on an individual level. When healthcare is socialized, everyone will need to subsidize unhealthy individuals. This will effectively make all the gains gotten from a stronger negotiating position irrelevant as people need to pay for the healthcare of those who otherwise would have to either improve their own lifestyles or stay ill.

And finally, the conclusion of making everyone pay for healthcare is already handled in a much better fashion on the market in the form of competitive health insurance. There is no need to replace private individuals pooling their resources with the state pooling resources. If anything, the problem is that private insurance pools are too restricted and that people cannot form

---

[40] The public health movement makes a critical error by trying to use the state to reduce poverty without making people accountable for their health.

groupings that they otherwise would have formed due to the incentives provided by the government. We can see this in the decline of fraternal societies[41] that used to provide healthcare with the assault on this type of organization by the government and the provision of healthcare by the government instead of these voluntary societies. Furthermore, it is often explicitly disallowed to form healthcare pools if they are not approved by the state which makes providing insurance impossible when it is not done in such a way that the state approves of. If the state is co-operating with pressure groups, this will necessarily mean the enrichment of the pressure groups at the cost of everyone else in society.

Thus, it is completely misguided to support the state providing healthcare on the basis presented above and this is why most people who advocate for universal healthcare are extremely misguided. They do nothing to actually address any problems but look at the simplest way out of a hard situation without actually looking into the causes. Furthermore, most of the rhetoric can be just as well be applied to any other resource on the market and it logically would imply full communism. If everyone needs boots and if boots are judged to be too expensive on the free market, the solution is obviously to require that boots are provided by the state and paid for by everyone.

There is a smart way to advocate for universal healthcare, but very few people do this as it is quite technical. This argument is to point out the issue with demand curves when it comes to

---

[41] This is further elaborated on in "Reactionary Liberty" by Robert Taylor.

healthcare, or to put it simply, it is to point out that no matter how much healthcare costs you have to pay for it because it's healthcare. You can't substitute healthcare for any other good once you're already ill and you can't look for healthcare providers who provide healthcare under the market price, this means that no matter how much healthcare costs, you have to pay that price or suffer the illness and the effects thereof. The demand curve is very vertical so the people who need healthcare will pay for it even if it costs absurd amounts of money. We can fix the price of healthcare all we want by introducing competition but there will always be this fundamental problem of people having to pay for healthcare even if it's expensive that will never truly reduce healthcare prices rapidly and efficiently on the market. At least as long as it is possible to form an oligopolistic system in which healthcare providers can cartelize to any extent, either explicitly or implicitly.

This is a good argument on its surface and makes intuitive economic sense, however, what the argument ignores is that it assumes that there are no new entrants on the market and that these new entrants will not greatly profit from a great reduction in prices. If new entrants onto the market charge greatly lesser prices than those currently providing healthcare on the market, they will have a massive opportunity to earn great profits due to their radical efficiency and customer friendly business model. Even though the old corporations are best off when they charge ridiculous amounts for services which do not justify the price, they are still held accountable when new entrants are allowed to enter the market and when they will inevitably suffer massive losses due to greatly reduced business. There can also not be any claim of natural monopoly when it comes to the market of healthcare as the costs to entry are mostly imposed by the government or a matter of human capital. The reason why healthcare is expensive is because the government has intentionally made it expensive. Without licensing monopolies by the American Medical Association, the competition would erode the importance of the demand curve. There are obviously specialized fields which require incredible amounts of capital investment for machinery, but these are only a small part of healthcare for all normal people.

A lot of the cost when it comes to healthcare is also due to copyright and the abuses thereof, which goes wholly contrary to the free market. Granting intellectual property is enabling monopolistic practices and will always ensure that the price of pharmaceuticals is as high as it can possibly be. If there was no inherent claim to the recipe of drugs we would see a massive reduction in prices when it comes to selling potentially life-saving medicine. This will result in lower profit margins for pharmaceutical companies, but ultimately mean that economic decentralization is incentivized. When it is no longer a viable method of profiteering to conduct in-house research and internalize all benefits without having the market be involved, medical research needs to be reduced to its own field. This greatly reduces the perverse incentives inherent in both producing and marketing medicine and will only lead to a higher standard of care for all. The major problem with the cost of healthcare is government enabled economic centralization, the solution is not centralizing healthcare more, but rather having the provision of healthcare be decentralized.

Insula Qui

Conservative Critiques

I – Culture

The problem of culture is the most poignant criticism of capitalism from both the left and the right, it is enough to make anyone with traditionalist or conservative leanings consider anti-capitalism as a plausible position to take. There are three ways in which capitalism could destroy culture and these are things that need to be addressed if we are to demonstrate that capitalism really does work. The first is that capitalism promotes degenerate behaviour, which we are seeing right now and which is thus very relevant to our inquiry into capitalism. The second is that capitalism causes degeneracy, that culture will be replaced by capital whenever there is capitalism. The third is related to the second in that capitalism may retain culture but it commodifies it instead of having culture be authentically appreciated as it is supposed to be.

The first complaint is that in a capitalist system degeneracy will always be increased. And this is reflected in reality, we can see megacorporations officially promote an agenda that aims for the destruction of the traditional family unit. We can also see people being denied a platform on social media for holding unfashionably regressive opinions. And this is not entirely the government requiring the corporations to be sufficiently progressive. This corruption is not the result of some trade union or any leftist establishment, but these are the very private companies who we wish to enable in the form of stopping government restrictions on the market. It seems as if this is an inescapable contradiction in our theory and the notion that capitalism will always be met with corporate leftism. There can never be a truly right-wing or conservative capitalism as the capitalists will never be right-wing or conservative[42]. Even if capitalism is not necessarily an agent for the destruction of society, capitalism is currently destroying culture and private businesses are as aligned with our enemies as the state is.

We can't say that leftism in capitalism is in any way a modern phenomenon, this occurrence was pointed out by the 20th-century fascists and the knowledge that capitalists go against traditional morality has been often described. We can't just wave this problem away by saying it's a condition of the current time. Even if it was just isolated into the worst of modernity, we see corporations adopting progressive opinions faster than solitary individuals do. For some reason, it seems as if within the corporate sphere leftism far outweightsany sort of conservative or traditional morality. The first thing that we need to confront is that corporations will uphold the status quo as long as they can. If corporations expect to profit the most when they espouse beliefs that are the most socially acceptable, the corporations will either promote socially acceptable opinions or remain completely apolitical. However, corporations can also expect to profit from pandering to revolutionary factions as revolutionary factions will use businesses if they see in those businesses allies. This means that corporations will hold the social positions of two groups, either the status quo or the revolutionaries

---

[42] We can also make the argument that capital flourishes in urban areas and as such capitalists will more likely be leftists. However, urban areas are incredibly subsidized by the government at the expense of rural areas. It could still be that corporate leftism has a root cause in government policy.

in society, just because they expect to profit most from these groups of people.

The revolutionaries don't have to be revolutionaries in the communist sense, they just need to be the people who want radical change within the socio-political structures of the populace the corporation works within. These revolutionaries are willing and looking for opportunities for platforms which align with their fringe and deeply held beliefs. Any savvy capitalist who sees this opportunity and is himself not steadfast in any philosophy will steep to their level and provide them with this ally in the form of his own business. The progressives will always have corporations that pander to them as they are expected to be beneficial to these corporations, but they must be relatively inoffensive in their platform or rhetoric, the corporations cannot pander to revolutionary agents who wish to do away with the corporation altogether.

The second position that the corporation can hold is pandering to the status quo, the corporation can simply reaffirm the beliefs of the majority and say what the corporation is supposed to say and expect a steady and certain stream of income from average people. When there are values that are considered decent, the corporation will benefit from appearing as if it is decent and thus benefit from reaffirming the status quo. Thus the only way a corporation can really be aligned with conservative ideas is if conservatism is the status quo or the management has deeply held beliefs that are conservative. This is because the conservatives can never be the radicals or the revolutionaries, conservatism as a philosophy is opposed to social change. There are of course radical variants of conservatism that are far more often aligned with the far-right rather than traditional conservatives. However, conservatism in itself does not provide a motive to ensure that corporations profit from pandering to conservatism. Furthermore, as western conservatism is influenced by Christianity, the conservatives do not look for a mortal utopia. This is a giant detriment as revolutionary movements are most often motivated by an unattainable yet appealing ideal.

This conundrum seems to be impossible to argue against until we notice that these corporations are owned by people who are rootless cosmopolitans. This can only lead us to the view that if we want to have capitalism in a productive manner, we need to do away with a society where rootless cosmopolitans are allowed to thrive. This is not a condemnation of capitalism in itself but rather simply a demonstration of how capitalism can easily fall to moral folly. Capitalism in itself does not prevent these attitudes from spreading so if there is to be conservative capitalism, it needs to be merged with community, faith, and morality.

Now we ought to address the notion that capitalism as a system causes degeneracy. The notion that in a system of liberty and exchange, people are better off following more materialist and hedonist paths in life rather than living in more traditional ways. Another related criticism is that the individualism inherent in capitalism removes from people any semblance of social responsibility and as such society would cease to be maintained as people are able to make individual and detached choices on the market. The first one of these is incredibly easy to address, capitalism doesn't cause any behaviour, but rather conforms to the behaviour present in society. If some behaviour is present in capitalism, it would also exist in every other economic system, if all other things are held equal. The immoral behaviour may be better hidden or less prevalent, however, the root causes are not eliminated by getting rid of capitalism as a system. Capitalism may enable all sorts of immorality, but capitalism does not cause immorality. In a similar way, capitalism enables every form of moral behaviour under the sun.

The second supposed fault of capitalism in the way it relates to culture is that individualism removes social responsibility. It thus creates people who are far more likely to forsake all tradition and all values and live according to more materialist or hedonist lines. To infer this requires misconstruing individualism in every possible way. Individualism is not selfishness to the detriment of the self, but rather just a way in which people are able to look out for those interests which allow them to live their proper life. This does not mean that these personal interests that allow for a proper life are necessarily or even likely to be anti-social. Most people would prefer to live in a society that they think promotes healthy and virtuous behaviour and most social people aim to be more healthy and more virtuous when it comes to their behaviour. Usually mentally healthy people also aim to take on some degree of responsibility for general virtue and advancing what they deem is proper.

Thus it is faulty to say that capitalist individualism would imply a disconnectedness from other people and that it would result in a breakdown of culture since people have a large individual interest in their culture. This criticism does apply to more urban and metropolitan areas where social bonds are largely broken and communities are less likely to form and stay stable and tight. However, capitalism doesn't imply at any point that most people should live in urban centres or metropolitan areas or that these areas should serve as residential areas where people live by choice and not to do business. I would expect a more capitalist society and free society to see a lot of deurbanization as open land is not withheld by the state and the costs of living in cities would be spread out and not internalized by the top marginal taxpayers.

The final point is one that is the hardest to refute and also the least relevant in the large scheme of things. This is that capitalism aims to resell culture to people and not to let the general public enjoy the culture of their nation independently. This commodification of culture would mean that capitalists nominally support a culture but practically just use the population to inflate their profits on the back of their constructed culture. But in order for this to work, people must first be alienated from their culture. If people are in touch with their own cultural heritage, then the capitalists cannot resell the culture of the people who already are passively connected to their own culture. Culture is a free good, it is abundant and does never deplete unless it is forgotten by all. However, in the case where there already has been an alienation from culture, capitalists can then fabricate a cultural identity and use that inauthentic identity to inflate their own profits without producing anything.

It is hard to say that this won't happen, but it's not a fault of capitalism, it is rather more of a virtue than anything else. When people are already robbed of their culture by internationalist, cosmopolitan and progressive forces, then capitalism is given free reign to provide them some purpose in a larger society. If we cannot defend our culture and if we cannot make culture something people can consistently appreciate, it's better if there are capitalists who will repackage and sell us culture than nothing at all. In this way, there is some semblance of an identity and of a social system and not just an empty void without any meaning and without any purpose. It may be a fabricated and commodified meaning, but it's better than nothing. In order to ensure the existence of authentic communities, we must prevent the decay of culture to prevent capitalist usurpation of culture.

II – Security

There are two facets to security that conservatives criticize when it comes to pure capitalism: economic security and security against violence. Conservatives infer from keynesian and socialist economics that there can be no true economic security under a completely free capitalism. Capitalism supposedly does not guarantee safety and is "wild". And even more egregious is to suppose that the capitalistic system can provide security for a nation or for an individual as the system of capitalism is corruptible and there can never really be a guarantee that each person and nation is protected if the state does not do so.

The second criticism is fairly easy to address, the state is also corruptible, to say that the market is incapable of providing security for individuals and for nations on the basis that it can do so in a way that has ill intentions, is to ignore how the state has been historically extremely malicious in the use of police and military. The state has historically dramatically failed at preventing wars and reducing crime in society. Thus, to say that capitalism cannot secure a person against violence is to ignore the fact that the state already does not do so. Furthermore, through empire, interventionism, and totalitarianism, the state has been a greater threat to personal safety than warlords could ever be. The state already provides a far worse quality of security than the private sector ever could and the only arguments that can be made are ones about free-riders, public goods, dominance hierarchies and universalism. None of these suppose that the market cannot provide security but simply that it is inefficient at doing so.

The notion of economic security and capitalism most often relate to three topics. The first are general economic collapses and problems within the organization of capital that will always fundamentally result in the economy being unstable. The second type of complaints are related to people losing their jobs or not having income for any reason that was not directly of their own doing and in essence suffering from greater economic realities. The third type of arguments related to economic insecurity are about the topic of imperfect or otherwise unwholesome goods. The most often proposed solutions to these are a counter-cyclical economic policy, a social safety net for those truly in need and regulation of goods and services to ensure quality. These all seem like noble goals and sensible solutions, but each one of these is deeply flawed.

The first type of complaint is based on the assumption that economies are naturally cyclical, and so a counter-cyclical policy must create an economy that is stable and without this degree of instability. However, this makes no sense, even if we assume that the economy is cyclical by nature, that doesn't lead us to believe that the economy will be fixed when we dump money into economic cycles. If the economy is cyclical, then attempting to solve the problems within the economy by recklessly throwing more money created by inflation into the economy can only serve to prolong the downturn or cause the existing downturn to worsen. This is precisely because the economy is supposedly cyclical, which in itself means that the economy will recuperate itself if left alone. And we can see this empirically too. Provided that economic collapse is inevitable, it doesn't mean that the solution is government interference.

Laissez-faire responses to economic downturns have almost always resulted in the economy eventually recuperating and doing so much more quickly than it does when the state interferes. The great depression and the great recession are the best examples of a counter-cyclical economic policy and also the worst recessions to ever happen. Thus, if the problem is with capitalism as an institution, then the solution too is provided by capitalism. Most economists also agree that a large cause of recessions is a problem of allocating capital. There is a narrow consensus that the problem lies somewhere within capital structures. So if the state interferes, the only thing it can do is provide people the funds to prolong the existence of these capital structures that have already failed while the free market would have to reorganize these structures if it wanted to be sustainable. No matter if the problem is with sticky wages, prolonged periods of production or too many people working the wrong job, allowing the economic system to retain the structures of capital by inflating the money supply is extremely counter-productive.

And this is just if we assume that business cycles are a part of the economy at large no matter what. It makes no difference if the problem is central banking, insufficient aggregate demand or a misallocation of real factors, business cycles cannot be fixed by government policy. To suggest otherwise would be naive and ignore the centuries of experience that we have accumulated by trying to fix business cycles with government intervention. Intervention into the business cycle has never produced the results that are desirable and have almost always left economies deeper in economic crisis without an end to the recession, economic security cannot be provided by the state. This may be a disillusioning fact and it may be something hard to accept, but it must be accepted if we want a reasonable policy when it comes to business cycles.

The other important issue is the notion that the people who are truly struggling require welfare and that it is a conservative principle to help out the weakest in society. It may be true that charity and caring for your own society are conservative principles. However, the fact pertinent to the matter is that any sort of social security or government aid only serves to replace charity. Thus it goes directly against everything conservatism stands for and can be considered directly against conservative values. The weakest in society do require help, but in the case where the state is responsible for providing this help, people seeking aid will aim to get it from the state.

Personal charity and strong communities should be the goal of conservatism. To tax away the income that people could have otherwise spent on helping others so the state can provide welfare is perverse. It is similarly perverse to replace the social safety net provided by community with the anti-social safety net provided by the state. If all types of welfare designed to help the poor were made into charitable organizations instead of remaining state-controlled redistributive schemes, individual persons could actually help people directly. These institutions still exist whilst the state has control over social aid. Furthermore, the attempt to wage a war on poverty resulted in the decisive victory of poverty, the state has proved itself completely incapable of providing help to those in need of it.

The state removes both the moral good of giving and the pressure for those receiving charity to actually use the charitable donations they received wisely. The state does not care about what people spend their money on when they receive it in the form of welfare as the state is not personally involved in the process of welfare. Various functionaries have no emotional attachment to the people who they are giving what amounts to free money. Having charity be done by actual individuals directly instead of through legal entities that do not exist materially will increase the moral stature of both the people giving and receiving charity. This is at least when compared to the situation where the state is responsible for securing a standard of living for all people. When the state provides charity, the people involved in the transactions are reduced to simply pawns of the state instead of actual humans.

Furthermore, removing personal involvement allows for various social ills caused by welfarism, people rely less on their families and communities and rather rely more on the state. Which allows them to be alienated from all environments that increase moral pressure and that provide grounding for individuals. Furthermore, this will always allow some people who do not need to get welfare to be able to receive welfare benefits. This would not happen under a system of private charity as then charity is personal, there is a degree of awareness to whom the charity goes to. This is simply because a bureaucracy is unable to accurately determine which persons deserve and which do not deserve the hard earned money of other people. There will always be those who do not need welfare who get welfare and those who are the most in need of welfare having to pay for the aid gotten by some other person.

The only real objection is to say that some people will not get the charity they need and are also not trustworthy enough to handle the delicate issue of providing for the poor. But how is the state any more qualified for ensuring the health and life of the poor than private individuals are? What is the special virtue of the state that allows for it to accurately determine who deserves aid and who does not? There is no answer to this question and there is no real life advantage to having the state be in control over what would be voluntary donations by and for individuals.

Then there is also the matter of regulatory systems to ensure that consumer products which people constantly use are not unwholesome and can be properly used without fear. It is often assumed that the regulation enacted by the government is designed to keep people safe. It is also assumed that this regulation is actually effective at protecting consumers without having significant negative consequences. It is simply a way consumers are protected from the potentially abusive corporations that otherwise would cut corners and risk the health and lives of the people who do business with them. But here we run into a hurdle when people know that they are risking their health and lives, they will only do so if they first are subject to extreme economic stress.

No matter how good asbestos may be for insulation, it is only used in exceedingly poor countries and industrial applications in those first world countries where it is legal. If people are already under extreme economic stress, it is impossible to afford better products. In all purchases there is an inherent trade between price and quality, with the problem of poor people buying sub-par products, regulations only serve as to deprive poor people of access to potentially dangerous products. But this does not mean poor people start suddenly buying better quality products, most likely, the poor would have nothing at all. Imagine that we required all people to only buy new cars due to safety concerns when it comes to used cars. This would not result in those who would otherwise be driving unsafe used cars now having safe cars, but rather this would only result in those who previously had unsafe cars to be carless. In any country where cars are a necessity, this can be much more dangerous.

And the profit motive itself will deal with dangers in products as the companies do not want to sell products that are problematic and would rather sell products that can actually turn a profit. A major force in putting the modern regulatory system into place was an incident in which toxic medicine was produced[43]. This was then used to prove how there needed to be a stronger central regulatory system that handled the quality control of new medications. However, what most stories do not account for is that the dangerous medication was immediately recalled when it was

---

[43] I am referring to the elixir sulfanilamide incident.

discovered that it was dangerous. Even though the medicine caused death, which is a very tragic situation, an emotional decision for central regulation might not be the objectively correct one. For all the deaths we see when there are mistakes with the production of medication, there are multiple we do not see when people are denied medicine due to regulatory problems. And it is not as if the regulatory frameworks within modern countries have prevented major problems. Since it is assumed that all products have been tested and are safe, people look out for their own well-being less than they ought to. There are still drugs that cause obvious and less obvious harm commonly used that are state-sanctioned. Crises in the pharmaceutical industry are still a regular aspect of life.

Even though the state is supposedly in charge of regulating and ensuring safety, we do see market alternatives for state agencies right now and they function much better than the state. This is true in the vast majority of cases. These enterprises can even make better guarantees that the product is safe. These private enterprises that regulate product quality are the agencies that provide testing before products enter the market and ensure that products are safe before those products ever get reviewed by the state. These private enterprises are much more efficient and can achieve results that are sufficient on their own. There is no need to assume that private companies would become defunct without the involvement of the state. The state only imposes a cost as necessary regulations would be taken care of by those market entities that currently provide regulatory compliance and unnecessary regulations are only a nuisance. Furthermore, in the age of internet, there is very little chance that a deficient product can ever remain on the market while remaining deficient. The problem of lacking information that could previously have caused people to buy faulty products can now be easily solved.

The whole network of private inspectors, laboratories and other various agencies that exist in order to ensure constant quality and regulatory compliance could completely overtake the state in providing wholesome and quality goods. To ignore this is to be completely and utterly irrational, there is no chance that there will be a rise in hazardous goods without the interference of the state. The only result of the state withdrawing from quality control can be the reduction in cost and regulatory burden that will allow for more efficient production of the same quality. That is unless the owners of all businesses simultaneously decide to start lacking any kind of sense and begin willingly destroying their own enterprise for some proof that they are theoretically able to provide unwholesome goods. Furthermore, those who are themselves damaged by consuming hazardous goods should be allowed to seek compensation for the damage done to them. Without the barrier of corporate immunity that is sanctioned by the state, those who unleash products that are potentially dangerous are likely to spend the entirety of their lives trying to pay off the damage that they caused. Personal responsibility is the answer when it comes to the sale of products.

III – Nationalism

Some nationalist groups assert that capitalism[44] in it's purest form must go against the nation as individual and international interests trump the interests of the national public. They assert that according to any good nationalist philosophy, the nation must be the primary agent and the individuals in the nation must be secondary and submit to the nation. Thus the individualistic system of capitalism must be restrained if there is to be any degree of nationalism. However, whenever the individualistic system of capitalism is restrained, it results in an impure version of capitalism or a fascistic economic system. There can supposedly be no philosophy that perfectly combines the two outlooks. If this is true, the logical extension is to regulate the markets and to make property rights weaker to defeat the individualistic nature of capitalism. This would be done in order to have the nation as the primary entity in society and facilitate the organization of society around the nation.

This is a seeming contradiction and it can only be solved in two ways, the first is to demonstrate how nationalism is not necessarily opposed to individualism. This goes contrary to the definitions of nationalism used by people who make the argument so this is a purely semantic debate on the surface. To avoid the semantic

---

44   There are "anti-capitalist" forms of nationalism that are still staunch believers in free markets and personal enterprise. We can argue over the terminology of capitalism and whether it intentionally refers to class warfare, but this chapter is simply for the discussion of how free markets and private property relate to nationalism.

debate we must demonstrate how the values of nationalism are not incompatible with the values of individualism. The second argument that can be made is that capitalism is not by necessity individualistic and one does not need to reduce freedom in enterprise for there to be a capitalism more oriented around the nation than the individual. I will be making both of these arguments, although I think the first one is much stronger than the second one in every way.

The first thing we need to assert is that nationalism does not need to take the nation as the primary unit in society and can take individuals as a primary unit in society. Nationalism, properly defined, is the valuation of the nation above the valuation of one's personal life. This does not require the nation to be more important in a social sense than the personal lives of the people in the nation. We can understand nationalism not as in the unit of the nation creating a valuation of itself above the private valuations of different persons, but rather as each person evaluating the nation above their own interests. We can also define nationalism as the nation being the primary value in society, that is the morality of a society being oriented around what benefits the nation and what does not.

If that is the case then there is also no need for the nation to be anything more than a supreme ideal the society strives toward. We can reduce this too to a matter of individual value judgements that place the nation above personal interests. We don't have to assert that individuals are unable to judge that their nation is more important to them than themselves, except when the national entity is institutionally superior to individuals. The decentralized approach to nationalism only requires that we acknowledge that nations as concepts are only as relevant as the people who create the nations as concepts. We must acknowledge that the nation is nothing eternal or transcendent, but rather something that individuals create through their own values and social interactions, there is nothing more to a nation than the people within that nation.

If the nationalists are also individuals who value the nation above themselves, then it would only be logical for nationalism to be a sort of individualism. This is as all individuals will make decisions oriented around the nation in one way or another. It's not like all individual decisions will by necessity go contrary to the nation and there is no need to assume that individual value judgements must in all cases be opposed to what is valuable to the nation and not conducive to nationalism. Individualism becomes trusting the individuals within the nation to orient their goals and morals around the nation and not around their shallow personal interests. And the proper way to ensure that the nation is respected is to increase the value of the nation for individuals.

This is hard to do, one must put countless hours into developing cultural works and forming communities to create a nation that is above just the petty affairs of each individual. There must be real effort put into the nation by the people that wish that their own nation was held in high regard. It's much simpler to do nothing and take a collectivistic approach which simply asserts that the nation is the primary unit in society and that the society must orient itself around the nation. It is much easier to force people to value the nation highly rather than to create reasons for why people should value the nation. We may strive for a nationalist ideal using collectivism or using individualism, however, taking the collectivist approach we must concede that the nation in itself is not valuable other than what is in the ideal. This is because we can't make the nation valuable ourselves and must force people to find value in the nation. This goes contrary to the principle of nationalism as an individualist endeavour, individualistic nationalism must be beneficial to the population that embraces nationalism as an ideal. Thus nationalism must create value in the nation.

We can call the collectivist approach fictitious nationalism and the individualist approach actuarial nationalism. The fictitious nationalism is oriented around creating a great image of the nation that is to be the centre of society. This aesthetic nationalism asserts that society ought to be devoted to the image of the nation. This sort of strategy is nothing more than creating a grand mirage through propaganda and public works. This nationalism may be immensely beautiful in the form of giant projects and an immense amount of investment into the aesthetics of the nation but it can't provide anything other than a fiction of a grand nation. The actuarial nationalism is built from the ground up to create a nation that people would willingly devote themselves to and a nation which plays into individual interests, unlike the fictitious nationalism. With the actuarial nationalism, there is nothing to be done other than decentralized action to create the best nation that can be created. There is no force required to build up a practical nation, only effort, time and resources.

This should firmly establish that every time a nationalist goes against individualism, it's not because he finds value in nations but precisely because he only finds value in the idea of nations. These nationalists who tell people about the horrors of individualism are conceding that individuals are not benefitted by the nation and that their nationalism is only oriented around the military class and the ruling class looking better. The people promoting fictitious nationalism tend to be useless and miserable in their private affairs and aim to achieve political power without any personal merit for their own deluded satisfaction. It's not worthwhile to listen to these people as their ideals are only dogmatic with no regard for the actual desires of the population. To follow the siren song of fictitious nationalism only oriented around the aesthetic of a nation is to submit yourself to the worst individuals in society.

This means that any nationalist that actually does aim to unselfishly improve the nation cannot be opposed to individualism on the principle that it harms the nation. A proper nationalist can be opposed to constant individuation that causes a deterioration in society and social alienation between persons. But the social placement of the individual above the nation would not be a problem if the nation was such a valuable entity that the individuals would value it above themselves without exogenous influences. This may seem complicated but when we look at social structures this becomes more obvious. In collectivistic nationalist societies, the nation has to be constructed from the top down by technocrats and dogmatists. When the nation is individualistic it becomes built from the bottom up, from the people who actually constitute that nation and not the people who want to use that nation for their own gain. Thus it may be claimed that individualism might result in selfishness and egocentrism, but those who claim this in regards to nationalism are ignoring the egocentric nature of centralization.

Furthermore, we can look at the deeper values of both individualism and nationalism. Individualism arises from moral principles of self-determination and freedom of association. This means that individualists simply want to be able to choose where their life goes and tie themselves down to whatever entity they want to be tied down to and nothing more. Nationalism arises from a desire to form unity, culture and order, a hierarchical structure which entails a unification of a people with a shared culture and heritage under the same society. This implies a focus on the society the culture creates and not a focus on what each individual themselves wants. This may again seem incompatible unless we use the logic that was used previously and assert that when the individuals in society choose to tie themselves down to the nation they can be allowed full self-determination and nationalism can still prevail. The only problem is when the nation does not offer enough value so that people would strive to protect their nation. Individuals will allocate their resources to the nation if the nation benefits the individuals who are within the nation.

The other argument to be had in regards to this topic is if capitalism is even inherently individualist, this comes down to the way we approach capitalism, either as a philosophical, political or economic system. And this is why the argument that capitalism is not individualist is weak when we consider both philosophical and political capitalism we find that capitalism is individualistic in the way that it opposes restrictions of the individual by the larger whole. And there is a great amount of overlap between the supporters of capitalism on a philosophical, political and economic level. The end result of this is that the supporters of capitalism will be to a certain degree individualists as they do not want to be subject to the larger central state or the group collective in general.

Economically speaking, capitalism is simply the private ownership of the means of production which infers the control of managerial actions being carried out on a decentralized scale and the profits being privately gathered. This is not individualist inherently but rather decentralist, capitalism as an economic ideal only implies that it is better to decentralize than to centralize. There is nothing inherent to nationalism that forces economic centralization to be the normal mode of operation. There can be a society that is completely oriented around the nation and where all economic operations are carried out in a decentralized manner.

IV – Selfishness

A lot of conservatives are drawn to the notion that capitalism inherently makes people selfish and as such capitalism should not be the primary method of organization and only can serve a secondary role to allocate less important resources. Since capitalism works for private profit and not for the public good, resources that provide for the public good cannot be provided by the capitalists as they work only for their own personal interest. Since the interest of the capitalist is not necessarily the interest of the people and the selfishness of the capitalist will make him necessarily only care for himself, this would result in a dystopia if capitalists controlled all industries. Furthermore, unrestrained capitalism will mean that people only look out for their own personal, narrow interest and not the social interest as a whole. Supposedly the state must take the role of looking out for the societal interest and restraining capitalism in order to do so.

There are multiple key problems with this line of reasoning. The unfounded assumptions within this form of logic can be largely divisible into four key assumptions. Capitalism causes selfishness, people will not look out for the public interest in capitalism, capitalists ignore the public interest and the state can look out for the public interest. In this way, we can properly organize and address what the supposed problems with capitalism are and can properly respond to each underlying assumption as they go far beyond what is demonstrated in the argument. If we do this we can properly address the claim that capitalism inherently results in some degree of selfishness as contrasted to the public good in the ideal economic system. It may be logical to call capitalism a greedy or a selfish system, but this is simply inaccurate.

The first problem is the assumption that there is something inherent in capitalism that makes people selfish. This argument has some actual merit as capitalism does not directly oppose selfishness and thus selfish people are able to openly prosper without flowery rhetoric in capitalism unlike in other economic systems. This means that capitalism must have something inherently that favours selfishness and that does not try to stop the social evil that is selfishness. But this ignores the fact that capitalism does not try to beat selfishness but rather redirects selfish urges to serve the interest of everyone else, people can form free economic relations that benefit everyone in selfish ways. Since, in a pure system of capitalism where property rights are respected, no one would enter a trade that they will lose out on[45], the capitalists must do their best to provide for the people who actually pay them. This also applies to every individual no matter where he lies in the relations within capitalism, his selfishness is only used to further everyone else.

So it may be true that capitalism doesn't do anything to directly counter selfishness, but rather, capitalism will inherently utilize selfishness that already exists to further the interests of everyone else. Since capitalistic relations must be based on mutual benefit as

---

[45] It is still a common misconception that trades ought to be equal. When in reality, when people trade, they get a step closer to the perfect allocation of resources, thus benefitting both sides.

the people within capitalism can have full control over their own resources, all selfishness must translate to an equivalent degree of selflessness in the form of helping others achieve their goals. The only way any person can profit from capitalism is if he does his best to make sure the greatest amount of other people have the greatest amount of benefit from capitalism. This ignores corporate hierarchy in which working within the corporation can produce better results than producing value for the corporation. But this is simply solved once the public-private partnership, the corporation, cannot hold powers that make it function far beyond the optimum size. When businesses are small, they cannot afford to give highly paid positions to inefficient employees.

Furthermore, there is nothing special about capitalists that makes them able to not have to abide by the necessity to serve others. Capitalists cannot profit from pure selfishness and thus they can not go against the public good as their profit comes from serving the public interest. Capitalists have no inherent market power that makes them able to do things that would harm the consumers that ultimately pay the capitalist. The only time where it is possible that the selfish interests of the capitalists can trump the interests of the public as a whole is when the property rights in society are eroded. When property rights are eroded, there can be transactions that are unfavourable to one or more parties. The capitalists will necessarily abuse this and create situations where their selfish interests can go against what the interests of the public are.

However, the answer to this is not additionally eroding property rights, but rather strengthening property rights. When this is done, all persons within that transaction once again have full control over their property in the transaction. The problem with the capitalist class abusing the rest of society is not the capitalist system but rather the political system that the capitalists are under. The system of selling off state power has the ability to erode property rights. Provided that the majority of people are not masochists, capitalists can do nothing other than offer valuable services on the free market. All profit the capitalists make is then correlating to the social good that the capitalists produce in the form of increasing the wealth in their own society.

And no self-respecting person would let the society that he is a part of become eroded under a system of capitalism. The additional prosperity and control over one's own property do not make it any less valuable that a person lives within a stable and pleasant community. Even if we assume that each person loses all their regard for their communities and that each person cannot even fathom helping the public good. It is still in their own interest to further the goals of their community as they themselves can internalize some of the good done by the community. Strong communities are good for everyone involved and everyone has an incentive to strengthen their community. Whether this incentive is stronger than the opportunity cost of focusing on the community depends on the individual scenario. But the incentive to maintain a strong community is constantly present. What this results in is that a capitalist system will necessarily have more resources devoted to communities in a decentralized manner.

A person does not magically lose their regard for their fellow man and want to become a hermit with no interest in the wider society as a whole. Humans are biologically extremely social beings and as such will always maintain interest in the society that they reside in. Because everyone biologically has the proclivity to engage in society, there will not be any significant lack of social relations when people are able to choose their own path in life. The only thing that will happen is that formal political relations will be replaced by more informal personal relations between the people in society and not between the state and society. This will necessarily cause increased strength in society as the people in society are directly engaging with one another and not indirectly through the political system.

And the political system itself can never be some selfless benefactor to the society in which it is in, the political system has people as selfish as anyone else within it and as such will be as selfish as any other entity. Furthermore, the political system does not need to make any profit or benefit anyone in any shape to retain it's continued position in society as there is nothing anyone can do to get rid of the political system. This means that the political system not only has selfishness but also enables selfishness far beyond what the capitalistic system ever could do. Since the political system does not punish selfishness individually or systematically, the political system can only be more selfish than any other agent on the economy. Furthermore, the people attracted to power are the people who want to use power for selfish gains and not for the public good. This means that not only does the state facilitate selfishness, it also attracts the people who want to be selfish. Whenever the state gains power, selfishness is increased. If the solution to selfishness is to increase state power, that solution contradicts itself.

V – Organizational Chaos

A big right-wing critique of capitalism is that capitalism inherently has some degree of organizational chaos. This is why you cannot have a capitalistic system where security, roads or any service provided by the government are privatized. Most people admit that this is not a problem with material things such as food or technology as the organizational chaos of capitalism does not result in significant disturbances due to the way the free market operates. However, if vital services were privatized, there can be no chance that they will be provided in a stable way under a purely market economy. This is why we need some degree of government regulation and government controlled industry, the free market is chaotic and not fit to be completely unrestrained.

But these people have absolutely no backing for their argument and never present any evidence other than absurd theories of mass murder. They have no logical reason to believe that capitalism is chaotic, but how could it not be? Capitalism is not ordered by anyone and thus must be disorderly. And since capitalism must be disorderly to a certain extent, there needs to be an agent of order to restrain capitalism. That agent, of course, being the state. Since there is no order without the state there can only be adverse effects of privatization and even worse in full marketization. Especially when these are large-scale public works projects or essential services. They need direct or indirect control by the state because otherwise there would be no visible order.

But this ignores how precisely everything in capitalism must be ordered to reach the final product. The surface level issues of violent disputes over property and irrational management are not present in most market activities. However, both of these modes of thinking and acting are extremely present in the government, and these are the main charges brought against capitalism. Someone could collect land and establish a monopoly or people will be so irrational as to greatly be a detriment to themselves. This is ignoring that the government has a monopoly on everything it provides and uses its monopoly irrationally. Any industry that is owned by the government or sold to one company for a pseudo-market solution is effectively monopolized. And the conservatives are in full support of this monopolization when it comes to anything the state does but this possibility of monopoly is enough to discredit the free market. We can only conclude that they just want a monopoly they have power over and what they really fear is the thought that someone else can treat them as they have been treating the world. Most normal people would not commit crimes as heinous as the statolatrous conservatives describe when talking about the potential of private defence, but they are all regularly committed by the state.

Furthermore, the state is a prime example of organizational chaos, it is organized based on nothing economic and rather the whims of the people within the state. The only goal that matters to the state is the amount of money the functionaries are able to collect, the only goal that matters to politicians is the votes they are able to get. There is no incentive to optimize the use of money for any other purpose than battling over votes or power. Thus the state will always be in an organizational chaos and as such we will always see tremendous bureaucracies and other government inefficiencies. There is no reason for the state to not have hundreds of thousands of pages worth of codes and laws and regulations, no one profits from optimizing that. In the same manner, no one benefits from making the government less involved in the lives of its citizens other than the citizens. The government only ever grows when it has well gone past its optimal size, assuming such a thing exists. However, a big problem is the supposed irrationality of private market actors. Private actors are able to make rational decisions faster than the government is able to make irrational decisions. It takes years of wasted time and money to come to a conclusion on a mundane vote and it takes only a few months for a private company to make much more vital decisions. Since some of these private decisions don't work out and since the private parties are actually responsible for themselves, people perceive these as abject failures born out of irrationality. But the government continues failed policies that have been failing for decades and it still has supporters as it has no need to answer for itself and can continue to be irrational.

There is no way a free market can even approximate the degree of irrationality within any government. But people are prideful, they don't admit mistakes when they don't have to. And the government almost never has to admit a single mistake. Thus, it can seem as if the government has made no mistakes and the mistakes it is making are just a part of life and not a failure. It's not as if government actors are more rational than market actors but rather that they are far less responsible for the consequences of their actions. We can even make the case that while the market punishes irrationality, the state rewards it.

Success on the free market is largely dependent upon how well people are able to predict the future. In economic terms, the more accurately a person can estimate future conditions, the more profit he is able to accumulate. This comes from the fact that supply and demand curves are constantly adjusting to new states of time and thus there is always a change in future desires and future prices. The more able one is in estimating how much of what people will be interested in, the more money he can make as his production will be more efficient. If one is irrational in current production, it will result in a direct loss of profits as there is a direct loss of customers with the costs remaining the same.

With the government, the opposite is true, when one is bad at predicting the future he can only use it to demonstrate how everything was worse than he initially thought or how something he proposed before had averted a disaster. From this irrationality, he can always get even more power if people fall for his rhetoric. Since demagoguery gets people elected, we can expect politicians to have a good sense of rhetoric and always being able to deflect their irrationality as a success. Furthermore, when something the government does is under budget the agency must find more things to do unless they want to risk losing the budget in the future. When something the government does is over their budget they can ask for an increase in budget and the initial investment will make increasing the budget an obvious choice.

And the government never loses customers or profits, everyone has to pay the government and use the services that the government provides. Not doing so means putting your life and property on the line and hoping that the government has mercy. There is no way in which one could spin the objective truth to imply that the people within the government are rational and the people in the market are irrational. Market activities have been able to deal with extremely complex questions when it comes to market research, engineering, advertising and whatever else one can imagine. To doubt that these people are irrational is to doubt that the market can even exist in a meaningful capacity and to assume that the government is by necessity wise is to ignore how the government demonstrably is not. Even the marvels of engineering the state has produced are all primarily aesthetic or military endeavours that would have been better if privatized.

There is still the blissful ignorance of assuming that the state is run by technical experts and professional politicians who know how to manage a country and who thus can provide the population with everything they need. This technocratic-popular government is purely a myth. The studies the government conducts are usually with very faulty methodology and only in very rare cases unbiased. The political experts are experts at enriching themselves to the detriment of all other people. The technocratic state only serves to enable the profit-seeking state, experts hired by the state are hired to validate the state and not to go against it.

And the government by design creates organizational chaos whenever it involves itself in the market. It's not only that the government is chaotic inside but also that the chaos of government spreads to the entirety of the economy. Nothing exists in isolation and the irrational government actions factor into the daily and long-term decision making of private individuals. Whenever the state offers a service freely to everyone or manages the economic actions of individuals, it causes false signals. People will always be deprived of choices with every piece of government regulation. This means that people have to choose less profitable paths in life over more profitable ones, this naturally causes a degree of irrationality in decision making. Furthermore, when services are offered at no cost or abundantly, people will use these services as if they have no cost or are abundant. When people have to spend their own money they do so reasonably, when everything is provided for them people do not care if they increase the costs of operation, but rather just want to use as much as they can. This can only be countered with a personal sense of morality but will inevitably lead to irrational and chaotic decisions.

Whenever people make irrational decisions, they have less money to spend on their rational decisions. Irrationality necessarily spreads out to the whole economy. Since taxes are funding irrational activities and since the government removes many rational activities, people are left with less money for lesser quality decisions. The entire organization of the economy by necessity is chaotic when the government is involved in people's lives to any degree. Still asserting that there is any great organizational chaos in capitalism is absurd.

And this complaint goes even further when we talk about replacing political systems with economic ones. The chorus of cries over how there would be warring territories and how there would be no sense of order are almost deafening. What these people conveniently forget is that in the democratic government there is what amounts to an overthrow of the government every few years. And this happens on multiple levels from the local to the municipal to the state to the superstate. Regime change is integral to democracy and the political chaos there could be if all land was owned privately is nothing compared to this. And unlike with politics, people actually have to maintain their own land, politicians only need to get votes from the people who maintain the land. Warmaking is bad for the sustaining of land, but amazing for gathering votes.

VI – Globalization

For some reason, there is an opposition to global economic integration among some more far-right conservatives. Supposedly this globalization is detrimental to national economies and leads to a form of global supranational capital which is inevitably in control of the national economy. Furthermore, free trade in itself is detrimental to workers of all countries and thus should be stopped. What makes this even worse is that domestic industries are often stunted by foreign industries. It seems as if so many problems with the economy are due to globalization and if we simply introduced a degree of autarky there would be more prosperity for everyone.

The first claim is sensible to a degree, the rest are blatantly absurd for the reasons I will discuss below. On the surface, it may seem obvious that global trade will privilege global entities over national entities as global entities can easily gain access to different nations. Since global corporations can integrate themselves without roots, the national enterprises will always be under economic assault whenever there is a globalized economy. Since we want to preserve nations and not have global states, we should also oppose unrestricted trade and focus on creating more national economic activity.

However, this should not be possible under an economic condition that is not created by a state-private partnership. It seems absurd that a company could become a business with no ties to any people of any nation. From a strictly business standpoint, this sort of unconnected multinational conglomerate is not bound to bring in a significant degree of profit as the owners of businesses need a population that they know. Trying to market a product to multiple populations with different desires will result in a lessening of profit in the long run. It seems like the strategy of internationalism in business is just an overall poor decision, yet we still see supranational corporations appearing in the global economy. What we quickly find out, however, is that most of these megacorporations are created from incentives provided by different governments or those governments themselves. The so-called predatory multinationals are not organically formed businesses on the free market. With the aid of the state, corporations can create a global market and surpass all national markets, this is not a market phenomenon but a political one.

The vision of free trade should be one of distinct co-operation and harmony of all nations through peaceful economic relations. The economic ties should all still be strictly between distinct national economies and not the current monstrous supranationals. It is also apparent that the only time businesses of a giant scale make economic sense is if governments are behind the corporation[46]. In a free market system, we would not see the formation of such enterprises that go against what individual nations do with their own economies. The most profitable strategy for a nation is integration into a global economy which allows all nations to take advantage of the advantages in their own condition.

---

[46]

It is often assumed that larger corporations will be more profitable, this is not true. When companies exceed their optimal size, available capital becomes used less efficiently and knowledge distribution becomes harder.

If all nations can trade peacefully, all nations can import and export in amounts that in the long-term would be equal in monetary terms when corrected for time preference. However, this would be met with an increase in the purchasing power of money as money is able to be spent for a greater variety of purposes, creating prosperity for all.

For governments, the cost that forming multinationals imposes is irrelevant as the government does not need to seek the approval of any party. It is not that the state wants to have peaceful economic relations to increase the amount of prosperity in their own country, but rather the state wants to increase their own influence. The way the state can increase the influence of the state in the field of trade is forming global supranational corporations. This form of economic imperialism will always increase the power of the state that is supporting the international corporation. It will be less profitable for all populations and more beneficial only for the owners of the corporation that the state sponsors and the state itself.

The problem with international capitalism, as with most anything, boils down to what the governments of the world have done and not something intrinsically wrong with the free market. It is not as if the ability to trade between countries has resulted in the vast amount of corruption, but simply the economic competition between governments has done so. The systems states create are not designed in such a way to be beneficial to people outside the globalist clique and the state. And here's the important distinction between economic globalization and political globalism. There is nothing that inherently ties an integrated world economy and an integrated world government together. There is nothing that requires economic imperialism when the matter is one of peaceful and mutually beneficial trade. There is no need for a government-run global economy or an international political system, the easiest thing is to just remove restrictions on trade and let people individually form trade relations that most benefit these individuals. By doing this all nations are eventually more wealthy.

The other side of the topic of globalization is the perceived problems caused to workers and businesses due to free trade, this is an issue riddled with incredibly deceptive claims and the deception is very easy to overlook. There are two main reasons why it is so easy to make people oppose free trade to preserve businesses and workers, first there is the fact of comparative advantage, second there is the dissipation of costs. With free trade some domestic industries will always be at a disadvantage towards some foreign industries, simply because foreign industries are more efficient, this also applies to workers. Because comparative advantage is a real economic phenomenon, what will eventually happen with free trade is that some domestic industries will go out of business and some workers will be displaced, this seems like an obvious negative.

But impressions can be deceptive, we ignore the other side of the coin, the industries that are more efficient than foreign industries. This is not a negative aspect of a world economy, but rather an important market signal telling the people involved in the economy to focus on the things that they do best and not on the things that are done poorly. The more efficient industries in distinct countries should be the most dominant industries as they are the most efficient on an international scale. We do not say that the United States does not grow enough black pepper because black pepper does not grow best in the United States. Why should we be against Asian countries producing a disproportionate amount of technology when they are the most disposed to producing this technology. Free trade allows all nations to partake of the wealth of other nations while in return using the resources they have to the best of their advantage eventually creating a better economy for everyone.

Furthermore, no one says that some municipality within their own nation is stealing jobs. There are very few people who blame Texas for joblessness in the Appalachian region even though Texas produces more oil which could potentially reduce demand for investing in Appalachian coal. If there were more coal-powered trains and less oil powered trains, it is probable that there would be more employment in Appalachia.

The important part here is that the benefits of free trade are not immediate, free trade has some pain involved as the industries that are more efficient somewhere else will suffer locally. Because seeing industries and workers suffer is an ugly sight, we may reach the conclusion that the problem is with free trade being somehow exploitative and detrimental to workers and industries. In actuality, what happens is that there are strong domestic signals on the market to produce something that isn't better produced elsewhere. But there's a problem when industries are protected from being bankrupt, everyone pays for it in small amounts. When workers need to retrain themselves and wasted capital needs to be salvaged, the cost is paid by a small number of people.

When there is a small interest group that is heavily affected by any issue that can be solved politically, the group will try to solve the issue politically. In the case of free trade, the suffering workers and businesses will seek to gain state aid in the form of protectionism instead of reutilizing capital and trying to get work in more efficient industries. The cost for this aid is dissipated across the entirety of the society, there's no cohesive organization to represent the victims who lost access to cheaper goods. Furthermore, protectionism also hurts workers in industries that are not protected as the workers lose their ability to effectively increase their position in their own industry, giving more power to the capitalist. This is because there is an artificial shortage of capital allocated to the industries which would be the most effective and this leaves a surplus of labour. Without there being a surplus of workers, the general labouring class would be in a much better position since the capitalist does not hold artificially scarce capital.

Economic Critiques

I – Irrationality and Knowledge

An often heard critique of capitalism is that, in reality, there is no rational allocation of resources on the free market. As such, there is a certain necessary degree of government intervention to prevent the problems that arise from market irrationality. Either these problems derive from moral critiques of capitalism or from a perspective that the macroeconomy is even in reality different and distinct from the microeconomy. The state control seemingly justified by irrationality is especially significant as it relates to monetary policy. Calling capitalism irrational can also result from a warped perspective when it comes to understanding economics and a personal attitude that is not conducive to views that can explain the problems within economies.

First, I will have to establish why it is that a capitalist economy can allocate resources in the most rational manner, as permitted by the available information. To start this we have to establish that humans have some degree of irrational behaviour, whether it be from a lapse of rationality or from a lack of ability to observe empirical evidence, humans do not act as perfectly rational creatures. If we were perfectly rational it would make no difference what economic system we use as economic decisions would boil down to simple mathematics, which would explain the optimal allocation of resources. Since we need to allocate resources, we are caught between two extremes, a completely rational allocation of resources and a completely irrational allocation of resources. These allow us to view economics as a "game" that aims to maximize the rationality in the allocation of resources. This means that we need to minimize irrationality.

How can we do this? The only real way is to increase the information in the economy, increase the capacity for obtaining rational thinking skills, lower social time preferences and provide incentives for acting rationally and disincentives for acting irrationality. However, when we do this we quickly can realize that popular government lies on the most irrational end of the spectrum and stateless capitalism lies on the most rational end. First, a pure market system puts all punishment for irrational actions on the person who performed those irrational actions and not on society or the state. A popular government by necessity socializes losses to an extent as each person will want their personal losses to be socialized, this increases the profitability of irrational actions.

Secondly, a popular government has systematic problems with time preference, when humans make democratic decisions they will not decide to aim for goals in the future because they are less relevant than problems in the present. Furthermore, when managing the money of other people, as the majority of tax revenue is from a minority of the population, it is not to the advantage of anyone to use that money in a prudent manner. Because this is true, any system of popular government will create a system where the class of people who decide the decisions of the government will prioritize the present over the future. This leaves the future uncertain and the people within the society are only able to reliably plan for the present. Each person in their own life does look after their own future as they will have to live it personally, but this is not the case in a group decision making process. When multiple persons have to reach a compromise they can't push for the things they want the least, this includes things in the future as they are not yet problems in the present. Group decisions thus will lead to a systematic focus on the present and a neglect of the future.

Furthermore, the executors of the group decision only have a temporary interest in the well-being of the society. Functionaries are not interested in what happens in the future, but rather focused on guaranteeing that the present condition is most favourable for the functionaries. The functionaries will, by political necessity, lose their power after enough time passes when they cease being elected or retire. Functionaries can only serve as temporary caretakers of whatever society they have power in. The people who execute the result of the decisions made by the populace through a vote will be incentivized to execute popular desires in such a way that it increases their own power and wealth in the present. The functionaries will be unable to make any decisions in the future as they will not have power in the future.

Furthermore, all people who have institutional authority benefit when the population is irrational and when the empirical observations of the people who supposedly control the government are distorted. When there are legitimized power structures in society that are based on a systematic dominion of the political class over the citizen class, the dominant political class will face great losses if the citizens do anything about their oppression. If the citizens had well-developed capabilities pertaining to rational thought and if the citizens were able to observe the empirical reality of the dominion by the political class, there would be issues for the political class. The citizens would immediately be opposed to being ruled over if the relationship between the political class and the citizenry doesn't become reciprocal. Since the political class wants to profit at the expense of the citizen class, the political class cannot afford for there to be actionable dissent within the citizen class. The moment that the hegemony of the ruling class is threatened, the political class will do anything to ensure the end of this dissent.

We can draw countless parallels that would equate anti-state libertarianism to anarchism. The anarchists want to abolish all hierarchy, whether it is political domination or the domination by men, whites or capitalists, but these parallels are tangential if best. Having a difference in sex, race or economic role is not necessarily a violent institution, rather these distinctions become similar power systems only if the state allows its violence to be used. Social power is not relevant to this discussion if the group exercising social power lacks the legal means to use violence against the group they exercise social power over. In a stateless society, there would be no group that can use legal violence against any other group so all group distinctions become irrelevant as anything other than a distinct form of social organization.

However, when a class of people has legal privileges over another class that allows the dominant class to suppress the unprivileged class with violence and intimidation, they will do so. Whether this manifests in corporations fighting unions by getting legal rights to use physical violence, men using the state to ban women from education or whites lynching blacks for speaking up[47]. This is also the case with the state gaining control over education, media, and academia, which all modern developed governments do and which all people in modern states are subject to.

The state will always tend to get a hegemony over the information available to the general public. When the state has this hegemony, the control of information will always be used for the benefit of the state and not of the citizenry as the state is the entity holding the hegemonic control over the society. The citizenry has no legal recourse against the state, the state does not need to fear any blowback for its actions. And this is by necessity true with any state as the state needs to exercise control over information to hold a monopoly on law. Manipulating knowledge is vital in order to guarantee that the state can create legislative law and organize society in the way the state wants to. The functionaries in control of the state will eventually be the ones who guarantee the results of democracy. Even if the democratic system is started for the sake of a just society, it always ends up cannibalizing itself.

This still is not an argument against the state, but rather holds to demonstrate how the state will always try to at least to some degree try to prevent access to information and the skills to process that information as the state does not benefit from people being rational

---

[47]

    In modern history there are also countless examples of unions using legal violence to fight against enterprises, women preventing men from getting an education and blacks using racial violence directed at whites.

and knowledgeable. When we look at the free market we see that each party aims to maximize the knowledge of each other party except for the case where there is an ongoing negotiation. When the people who you do business with are the most knowledgeable, you can usually expect business relations to be more efficient and more productive. When the education system is held accountable for the education they provide and cannot leverage a bad quality of education for more money, they too will have to put more focus into providing quality education. When parents are given a choice on how their children are educated, they will have to take personal care so that the education their children receive is of quality. Ultimately in most relations without using systems of force, there is an increase in the drive for better education. Capitalists want better-educated workers, men want better-educated wives, if only for the sake of better home economics and whites have more use for well-educated blacks than for poorly educated blacks.

However, the education in any organic stateless society will not be the universal and hierarchical education provided by the state. But more likely specialized education for the specific field the education is necessary for or a lower amount of universalized education followed by specialized education. This is simply how education has been in history. However, this is not inherently worse and will allow people to better develop their skills of rationality and observation alongside a wider branch of specialized knowledge. Even classical education could be brought back for the sake of fostering intellectualism in the most intelligent. If the smartest in society started learning according to the trivium and the quadrivium before moving onto philosophy, it could produce a new enlightenment solely by itself.

Furthermore, the decentralized process of making decisions in the market creates a condition that minimizes the impact of all irrational decisions. When decisions are made in a centralized manner either democratically or autocratically, the mistakes that come from irrationality ripple through the whole society. When people make their own mistakes, the impact of each irrational decision is minimized and most people are unaffected by slight miscalculations. Mistakes become only systematic inefficiency instead of creating crises. Contrary to the market order, when centralized decision making fails, it affects all people who are under the influence of the central agency. Furthermore, decentralized agents have more information on the subject matter they are dealing with than the centralized agents could, there is no capacity to accurately judge subjective valuations on a centralized level no matter how objectively it could function in theory. Furthermore, subjective valuations can only evaluate empirical information, this too is absent from the knowledge base of the central agency. When there is not enough information, there is no hope that the end result could be anything other than irrational.

The next problem we need to address is the moral criticism that capitalism is by necessity irrational and that capitalism should be abolished as it cannot provide a rational economy. This problem usually relates to the fact that capitalism allows for wealth inequality, does not provide people with the goods they need for life or is simply a mode of production that has no basis in reality and should be replaced by a more just and natural communist mode of production. The first argument is usually the most poignant as the proponents of it can flaunt statistics that say that eight people have more wealth than the bottom 50% of the world's population. This seems absurd and irrational until you realize that the bottom 50% of the world's population still live in huts without advancing beyond the eras of history that the rest of us have gone through.

People who are still stuck in subsistence farming have no wealth at all, the only remedy to this is the increase of capitalism. It is odd that the countries in which this sort of life is still practised all tend to be overwhelmingly economically restrictive and not very inclined towards the free market. Whether this is cultural, biological or institutional bears little to no relevance. The people who work only for themselves and consume what they produce, rationally do not deserve any more wealth than they already have. They make no wider contributions to the rest of society and as such are rightfully relegated to poverty. And even when we look at the most wealthy businessmen, we can see that most of them have connections to the state. The majority of the richest people in the world did not gain their fortune from pure free market capitalism. And the few who actually did gain their wealth from the market have provided life-changing services or products. The people who use these revolutionary products profit from them greatly and thus the entrepreneurs that ushered in the economic change deserve the money they have. Unless the state is intentionally redistributing wealth from the poor to the rich, this remains true.

The second perceived irrationality is that capitalism does not provide for everyone simply because they're humans and that this is irrational for some reason, but it's extremely rational. "If any would not work, neither should he eat" is a simple principle, and in a capitalist system, it is applied systematically. There is still the question of people too poor to feed their families even though they are working or people who can't afford basic necessities no matter how much they work. This is usually resolved by tracing the cause of poverty back to something the individual themselves is responsible for, such as alcoholism, single motherhood, a worthless education or something the state did. People who do not waste money, who have skills that can be applied, know how to communicate with other people and who don't strive to live beyond their means are not usually impoverished for their entire lives.

And finally, there is the argument that there is no concrete human nature and that the capitalist system is only an unjust system not backed by anything other than the preceding material and historical conditions. There is no eternal truth to capitalism but simply capitalism is the manifestation of class conflict in an industrial society. Furthermore, there should be a similar revolution in regards to capitalism as there was when feudalism was defeated. The industrial economy has given in for the sake of the modern economy, capitalism is no longer an efficient system. Thus, it is irrational for capitalism to keep functioning as there is no more need for capitalism and there are no eternal truths inherent in the capitalist system.

But this is a debate largely on terms that contradict themselves. When capitalism is only a manifestation of the industrial economy, why have there been capitalistic systems of organization in various agricultural economies. Mercantilism and feudalism was not the universal condition of mankind before capitalism. Furthermore, if there is no inherent nature to humans, how do different modes of production create different patterns of behaviour and organization, why do humans respond to material incentives if it is the case that there is no nature to humans.

There is also the problem that some people may have with perspective when examining capitalism. A lot of people think that since all decisions made were not correct or that they would have themselves made different decisions were they capitalists, capitalism must be irrational. The temporarily embarrassed central planners think that if they were only in control of the state, they could build a utopian society that is better than any other society. These people tend to be well educated and somewhat intelligent so it makes sense for them to have the attitude of control and subjugation as they have an inflated importance of their own ego and their own ability. If the would-be general secretaries really were this much more rational they could easily find themselves in managerial positions. But this is only true if they had chosen to pursue economically productive paths in life. They could be the ones who are making the decisions for the economy, the only thing stopping them is their own inability to properly work and produce value.

And finally there is the notion that individuals are rational in the microeconomy but irrational in the macroeconomy, individuals may make mistakes when it comes to the way they organize their own lives but mostly they organize rationally. However, these decisions do not take into account the larger scale of social organization and economics and thus these decisions will result in larger scale irrationality as the optimal use of resources is not the same on the small and the large levels. This means that we need a rational government to use technocratic methods to organize the larger society and the economy so individual decisions will not create an outcome that is worse than what would otherwise have been. This logic is implicitly embraced in a lot of modern economics and the fact that it is is a travesty of the highest order.

First, it makes the greatest intellectual failure by assuming that the state is required to prevent irrationality when any other entity could make society more rational on a purely voluntary basis without any involvement by the state. If the macroeconomy is relevant to people's lives they would want to prevent failures in the macroeconomy and create economic demand to organize society in a better fashion. This can be voluntarily capitalized on to improve the quality of society. If the supposed macroeconomy bears no relevance to the personal lives of people, then the people who benefit from the macroeconomy would organize to prevent disasters even if the state had no involvement in the economy. Involving the state would be inefficient as voluntary collections of people are better at making rational decisions than the central state is. Furthermore, this sort of central planning assumes that the decisions people make in their personal lives will cause failures in the macroeconomy. This is only true insofar as there are structures that allow for costs to be socialized across the entirety of a given economy. These structures only exist when some industries are so involved with the government that the government can socialize the losses from those industries.

When people decide how much products they want to consume, they do not affect other people by these decisions and do not change the macroeconomic conditions by changing their bread habits. If everyone ceases to want bread, then bread production should be ceased as people have no longer a need for bread, if the demand for bread declines there should be a similar decline in the production of bread. When the propensity to consume decreases, then there should be a decrease in production on a large scale and this only causes economic gluts when losses are socialized and businesses who default on their obligations are not held individually responsible for what they need to compensate their debtors and clients. However, there is no need for the propensity to consume to be organically and periodically reduced on the free market as most people want to use their money to either invest or consume. The chance that there could even be a situation where people suddenly stop wanting anything and leave their money completely idle is not likely. People can wait until the future to spend their money, but this is simply shifting consumption forward in time and not a reduction in overall consumption.

And finally, the greatest mistake is assuming that there even is such a thing as the macroeconomy and that there is a meaningful difference in economics with the change of the size of the economy that it analyzes. We can aggregate to an extent what people do in the economy to have a point of comparison, but this is not a scientific measure as it cannot describe anything real and can only show how people function according to the characteristics required of being a part of that aggregate. In reality, there are only different actions by individuals and intersecting microeconomic phenomena that lead to different results on larger scales. The only macroeconomy that exists, exists purely on paper and is not reflected in reality.

II – Instability

There are two reasons why anti-capitalist economists think that capitalism has inherent instability which must result in crisis or collapse of one type or another. These reasons for why capitalism must collapse also affect everyday relations under capitalism and will necessarily contribute to capitalism being a burdensome system. The first issue is that people are allowed to make their own decisions without any centralized control, this has fallen out of fashion so I will not be addressing the full socialist idea, but rather the idea that people need some degree of economic control in some areas to prevent instability. This is done using state control as simply a conduit for the sake of making better decisions. And secondly that the relations to capital that put the capitalists in privileged and more powerful positions cause an inherent instability as the interests of the workers and the capitalists are contradictory. As such the economy will be unstable as it is aiming to solve this contradiction.

There is also a third critique that is more prevalent and even used by pro-capitalist thinkers. This is the notion that capitalism is unstable, but this is not an entirely negative process as creative destruction ensures innovation and proper economic advancement. This is only a criticism insofar as it is a misconception that makes capitalism seem inherently dangerous due to people being free, it is more subtle but also important. To admit that capitalism must be destructive in order to be creative is to spread an image contradictory to the free economy.

The first anti-capitalist criticism is that since capitalism is unplanned in one way or another, it cannot create a society where people can produce in an orderly fashion. As such, capitalism must result in an unstable economy where people try to produce things that do not need to be produced to outcompete others. Furthermore and worst of all, capitalism will result in people doing various things that are wholly unnecessary in the so-called anarchy of production. If everyone fell in line and functioned according to one plan, these problems would be avoided and there would be no needless waste caused by the inherent instability in free market competition. There would also be a much more efficient allocation of resources as the competitive capitalists would be replaced by collaborative socialists. Supply and demand are not good answers to solve the problem of economic distribution because supply and demand cannot account for everything. People are more than just agents in the economy, they act according to their position to capital and not as idealized agents on the market. To allocate resources according to the monetary value of the individuals in an economy is to end up with an unjust distribution of wealth

But this logic is absurd and thankfully most people have understood just how absurd this is, the problem with capitalism is not that it's unplanned. No matter the faults of capitalism could be, the market economy is very meticulously planned by every actor within the market. However, capitalism is not planned by a central agency, the plans of individuals are as solid as the plans of socialist agencies, just no person or oligarchy can single-handedly decide what these plans are. Capitalism, in essence, synthesizes the various plans in a society into a cohesive order of production. This is of course unless there has already been a central planner established without the complete abolition of property rights. Central planning is present in the modern economy in the form corporate oligarchies or technocrats who meddle in the monetary system. They are central planners as much as the socialist hero with his five-year plan is.

Under a free market, individual plans do not contradict one another, but rather co-ordinate with as many other people as possible. Planning within a market system is simply accounting for the behaviours of other people and ensuring that your decisions complement theirs in such a manner that you can earn a profit. Profit is based on mutual exchange so every person within a free market must plan for all exchanges they are likely to commit or do regularly commit. Thus if market actors want to ever succeed in the market, they must be able to co-ordinate their plans with the plans of others. Capitalism is as collaborative if not more than socialism is, this is because everyone within capitalism must ensure that their plans line up with other people.

Under a regime of socialism, planning becomes impossible when it comes to personal transactions, this is precisely because of the rigidity that arises from central planning. When people cannot co-operate in their predictive powers without ulterior motives through the price system, there is no way to internalize the profit caused by planning. When there can be no profit derived from proper planning, there can only be an increase in improper planning. Planning in socialism is a utopian notion which assumes that the central government has the proper plan which will certainly be reflected in reality. This has never been the case and will never be the case, the central socialist state erring in it's planning will cause an overarching social loss. All attempts to socialize the benefits of planning have resulted in socializing the costs of poor planning. The reason why becomes obvious once we realize that the central government simply will always lack the necessary information to plan. The capitalist economy is meticulously planned while the socialist economy is in a state of perpetual chaos.

The only people who believe that there should still be some form of central planning are very fringe socialists. The purported logic of central planning has completely fallen out of favour so there seems to be no impetus to discuss the problem of central planning. But this is a wrong approach as the underlying assumptions are still as present as ever, just in a very minute capacity in a modified context. As mentioned above, it is important to point out that to oppose central planning without opposing corporate oligarchies or centrally planned monetary policy makes no sense. There is functionally no difference between a narrow group of corporate interests with political power and a singular political party or group of technocrats with access to the same political power. All the faults of central planning are present in the so-called "corporatist" system, which often characterizes the modern economy.

As state chartered corporations, especially as they relate to entertainment, information technology, and banking, grow in influence, they are able to singlehandedly plan the direction of their sector of the economy. Shielded by patents, corporate charters, and intellectual property, these corporations have managed to corner the market without any personal merit. The modern consumer culture is planned by the controlling corporations, having the corporations be in control of the economy leads a consumer to either accept what they put out or nothing at all. This leads to perpetual shortages and surpluses when they are the least desirable. The nexuses of culture and money have become centralized and have had the world suffer under their regime of central planning. Although the profit motive might alleviate some of these ills in the short term, when taking a broader view we can see how destructive these state-chartered corporations have become.

Furthermore, when monetary policy is concentrated within a national bank, it results in the monetary policy only being within the domain of that bank. This results in the banks having the sole control of the decisions made as they relate to the printing of money. As the bank is in control of the value of money, the bank will be in control of the entire economy. Since the bank plans the value of the money into the future, the planning of the bank will be as faulty as the planning of any socialist bureau. The bank will externalize the social losses caused by its faulty planning and will force all within the economy to suffer from the instability that chaos causes.

Even though barely anyone wants to achieve full socialism, many people still claim that individuals are incapable of planning in one way or another and as such the state must do it for them. The most common example of this is the almost ever-present fact of state-pensions. In most developed countries, the state controls some amount of money people get while retired and the collection of that money via various taxes, this is more often than not compulsory. The justification for forcefully collecting pension money is that people themselves would not save enough. But this is logic that is as poor as the logic that is used to support the form of authoritarian socialism in which all factors of the economy are centrally planned. There is no great folly within the system of individuals saving as much as they themselves save and then suffering the consequences if they have made a mistake, central planning here does not help anyone.

But when confronted with such an emotional issue, it is hard to understand why central planning no longer works when the stakes are old people. When it comes to emotional issues, central planning could be desirable so as it could avoid the social ill of people feeling sad about it, but this is very flawed logic. The answer is plainly one of information, people themselves are the best aware of their needs and no one else could possibly understand what they want as well as they do. Whenever the state aims to centrally plan something, it will always lack information and have results that do more harm than they do good. Each person has hundreds of thousands of desires and plans, which they can keep track of only because so much of these are instinctual. Each person focuses on certain things from time to time more than average. And even worse, not only is it necessary to keep count of desires and motivations, it is also vital to organize these desires in points of time when they will vary in intensity. This leaves individuals the ability to keep track of everything they want and individuals alone are able to plan for the things that they themselves value. This applies equally to simple affairs and grand overarching goals.

However, we cannot understand the desires which other people have relating to their lives in the same way we can for ourselves, this is a fundamental problem of knowledge. No-one can know the self perfectly from an outside perspective, it is impossible to make decisions for others that are better than the decisions they would have made for themselves. A lot of desires and wants are also irrational and cannot be categorized by central planners in such a way that they would logically make sense. Although these wants are not rational, they result in a net positive for all members of a society as they produce subjective value. In essence, although they are not rational in the same way as maintaining proper nutrition is rational, they are beneficial. Irrationality is a fundamental factor in human life and should not be avoided.

Furthermore, it is impossible to keep proper track of information itself in a centralized manner. Decentralized entities can use information to a much greater degree due to specialization, each person is fully specialized into their own private affairs. These and many more things contribute to the inability of the state to ever undertake central planning and actually succeed at having positive results. Even with things such as retirement, we cannot resort to central planning to solve real issues. Involuntary decisions made by central planners will always bring unintended consequences.

Then there is also the matter of the different interests within capitalism causing instability. Workers want things that are good for the workers and capitalists want things that are good for capitalists. Thus there must be an unstable system as there is no mutual agreement between the social classes. Capitalists want capital to be as valuable as possible and workers want labour to be as valuable as possible, the more valuable capital is, the less valuable labour is in comparison and vice versa. This results in the capitalists and the workers being in a fundamental conflict over how the economy operates. The class conflict will always fundamentally destabilize the economy resulting in either capitalists or workers centralizing power. The same can be said whenever there are distinct groups with differing interests as it relates to economic organization and the only way to reconcile these groups is to solve the conflict in one way or another. This does not apply to any normal market for goods, as trading goods is a fundamental trade for a title of ownership. Both parties want to trade titles, which will result in most of these trades being desirable or the bankruptcy of the enterprise that cannot offer desirable trades.

But the logic of capitalist class conflict lies on the fundamental assumption that differing interests must create instability and that this instability can be better solved by the abolition of the market economy. The fact of the matter is that the market is simply a process by which group differences can be solved and negotiated and the market is the way by which different groups can peacefully co-operate. Using the market is not creating an unstable condition, but rather fixing a condition that would otherwise have been unstable. The market is based on people exchanging goods and services at prices they deem to be worthwhile, and this basic principle has wide-reaching implications. Market decisions are made by evaluating all options available to distinct individuals and as such create a way for each person to choose the path that most benefits them.

There are thus only two ways to solve group differences, the first is to either completely separate as groups and remove the parasitic elements if there is no reconciliation between these groups. The second is to reconcile these differences in the form of a contract that is agreeable to both parties, there is no way to create instability by using market means. Instability is created only when the groups with different interests struggle to gain control over the state and when these groups are not forced to solve their differences via the market. A power struggle results in unstable societies and economies, peaceful contracts are a stabilizing force for the advancement of mankind. The only reason capitalism is unstable is due to politics being unstable, the faults of the political economy lie solely within the political. And since the free market is a way in which all people aim to maximize the quality of their lives, these contracts will be the best available contracts. Thus, the instability of class struggle under capitalism is diverted into peaceful collaboration. The conflict is utilized to ensure a better quality of life for the worker and the capitalist.

And finally, from the pro-capitalism side, there is the notion that capitalism engages in a form of creative destruction or some other process in which by instability there is innovation and economic growth. The old must be constantly in conflict with the new and that there needs to be some form of destruction to create. This is a very popular way to explain capitalism, the destruction of the old in favour of the new and the inevitable march of modernity. But this is misguided for a great number of reasons. First, there is no benefit to destroying anything in capitalism, there is no reason to destroy things that function in favour of creating things that are even better. However, what capitalism does is naturally grow and through this process of growth everything old will become repurposed. The small plants in a rainforest rot to feed the big plants, which will eventually die and rot again to make room for a new generation of small plants. The same is true in capitalism. The causal relations of capitalism are greatly distorted in order to make it appear as if there is some form of destruction within the capitalist economy when there is actually none present.

This is not a constant revolutionizing of industry that completely reworks the old system, but rather the old system becoming defunct with the growth of the new. Capitalism is not a sweeping revolution but rather the ability for everyone to increase their own position in the economy. Capitalistic advancement is not a wild process with ups and downs but in the purest form a linear growth that allows for increased efficiency and increased quality from what previously was worse. It does not destroy the old without any heed to the consequences but rather the old gets retired once the new has demonstrated the efficiency that the new can provide. Only when there has first been creation, there is repurposing and "destruction". This is not merely an issue of semantics but of a fundamental understanding of capitalism. It is not instability that causes growth, but rather the stable increase in human society. It is not wild stagnation followed by the purge of the old, but rather the new growing upon the old which too grew upon the last generation.

III – Sustainability

For a multitude of reasons economists and communists both think that capitalism will fail at points or altogether because it's not sustainable. Capitalism may work in the moment but it's not going to work in the future, for one reason or another capitalism will suffer a self-imposed injury and thus stop existing or properly functioning. I will be focusing on the economic case for why this misguided and why there is no actual reason to believe that capitalism is not sustainable.

First, we need to understand intertemporal utility or, as austrian economists call this concept, time preference. This notion is a simple one, people value goods in the future less than they value goods in the present. People don't like waiting, provided that they don't have to wait, as such, everyone would prefer to have an equivalent good in the present rather than in the future. For example, if given a choice between an apple a week in the future or an apple today, all other things equal, any person will choose an apple today. This applies to larger issues such as land use, capital structures, and workplace relations.

It also applies to land use and explains why capitalism can be sustained without depleting land. If people want to use their land they have to ensure that the uses in the future do not outweigh the uses in the present. If the land-owners do not ensure potential future profits, they will themselves impose a tremendous opportunity cost. If it is expected that a land will bring a massive profit tomorrow, it is not advantageous to sell it for a minor profit today.

Capitalists are not idiots, we cannot assume that they do not see the future value of goods. So it may seem that capitalists are greedy and exploit the resources of the earth, but this is simply because the utility of these goods is greater in the present due to the effects of time on the value of goods. Thus it can easily appear as if available resources are used at an unsustainable level when in actuality they are used close to the optimal level considering the intertemporal utility of these resources. And we need to also consider that capitalists are the only people who truly have an incentive to preserve their resources. They hold the rights to their property in the present and also in the future, if the property loses its value then the capitalists cannot use it for profit any longer. If capitalism was driven to unsustainability by the fact that it exploits natural resources, it can only be due to a systemic lack of knowledge about the state and availability of these resources. Or it could be true that some resource has better alternatives and thus the capitalists have no reason to preserve future value as the value will decrease due to the increased pressure by the alternative product. If this is the case we should cheer the "exploitation" of natural resources as it gives us cheaper goods without any cost to the future.

Then there is also the claim that relations between capital and labour make capitalism inherently unsustainable. Most of these originate from the largely defunct school of marxian economics but this relates to the last topic and is useful to know. What the marxians believe is that due to capitalists getting profit without doing physical labour they must be exploiting workers. This arrangement of things is unsustainable as the workers will demand that they get the value of their labour and thus capitalists will have no choice other than to monopolize to keep their hegemony. If capitalists are unable to monopolize further, then capitalism must stop functioning as capitalists cannot resist the traction labour will get for itself to topple capitalism. This relies on the notion that capitalists hold a perpetual hegemony over capital. The truth is that if socialist organizational units wanted to establish production they could do so right now. If workers created all value, they would not need capitalists and socialism would not need a revolution. However, workers having to provide their own food and shelter before their production can sustain their lives will result in a lack of people willing to establish socialist enterprises. Under socialism, this problem becomes systematic instead of incidental.

The least controversial of the proofs when it comes to the instability of capitalism is the theory that capital structures will inherently turn out to be unsustainable within any capitalist economy and as such there will be perpetual recessions. This usually is facilitated by a demonstration about how capitalism is supposedly a system where irrationality holds some degree of sway. Due to irrationality, we will see system-wide recessions regularly when the factors of capital are managed in a decentralized manner. The most popular explanations for these recessions are that they either happen because real factors change or are misallocated, or the keynesian explanation which I will discuss in depth[48]. The notion that real factors become misallocated is not a condemnation of capitalism, but simply the demonstration that the market economy is confronted with immutable reality where people make mistakes.

The keynesian explanation starts off by asserting that in an industrial economy there is a phenomenon of sticky wages. Wages cannot adjust as fast as the value that workers produce and there will perpetually be problems with changing wage rates to fit productivity. Because wages are sticky, the economy will not consistently be at full employment. If there is no full employment, then there is some degree of deficit in overall demand which creates a problem. Companies will not have enough capital to sustain themselves. Because companies cannot sustain themselves, they will go out of business and if they go out of business then the problem only intensifies with other companies going out of business due to there being even less aggregate demand. This creates a system-wide shock where the economy is in a recession and the only way to fix this is with government intervention where there is new money created to restart the economy by creating additional demand. In the worst case scenario, the economy might even require government spending to grow in real terms. This falls flat at every point.

The reasoning makes multiple assertions which are all backed by flawed logic. First that wages must be sticky and the stickiness of wages affects aggregate demand due to workers not accepting

---

[48] The author does not believe that either is true but rather subscribes to the austrian business cycle theory.

pay cuts for one reason or another. But this cannot stand up under the slightest scrutiny. It may be hard to accept lower wages, but there is no reason that this needs to imply systematic underemployment. If there is a large amount of labour that is not marginally useful at the current wage level, it only means that these people can be put to work at a reduced wage level and does not need to imply that the existing workers will have their pay cut. There must be some other reason for underemployment which is not necessarily wages being sticky[49]. Furthermore, there is no need to expect the general wage level to be on a downward trend unless there is a deflationary currency with no increase in productivity[50]. With the advancement of the economy and a stable or inflationary currency the stickiness of wages should never be relevant. And in the modern economy, which has had all of the worst depressions, the currency has not been deflationary, but rather inflationary. Thus inflationary currency does not prevent underemployment by managing to eliminate the problems caused by the stickiness of wages. If sticky wages were the cause of prolonged depressions, the great depression and the great recession should have both been averted by the inflationary dollar.

---

[49] And if wages are sticky on such a wide scale, they will be sticky due to the involvement of labour unions.

[50] I would still contend that wage rates remain similar and do not fall with a deflationary currency as productivity must increase at least as fast or faster as the currency deflates due to deflation reflecting an advancement in the state of the economy.

The keynesians then answer by contending that underemployment can be a result of a lack of aggregate demand, so even if the economy would theoretically be capable of adjusting wages, there are still problems as everyone cannot be hired profitably. There is not enough demand in the system to produce goods to the extent that is physically possible, thus workers will be underemployed. This reduction in demand may be due to a long run pessimism due to the increase in the cost of capital goods which is balanced out by the increased investment in more optimistic times. This increase in the cost of capital goods then explains why it is possible that it really is the fault of capitalism that we experience recessions and the government does have to increase demand to make capitalism sustainable. If there is no impetus to invest in capital goods even when the economy is gripped by pessimism, the depression will never go away on its own.

But this is the result of macroeconomic thinking and assumes that we can view the economy in aggregates. This makes no sense when we consider individual business relations. There is no reason for the lack of immediate increase of investment into capital goods to cause a shortage of capital goods. Rather there can be substitutes for the capital goods and we see this happening in the real world. When capital goods are lacking people just use lesser capital goods and don't stop using capital goods. This may be less efficient but is not enough to cause the large crisis that we see in recessions. It is more profitable to operate at a loss than to burden yourself with the costs of a failed business. If bankruptcy is socialized, this may change, but it is then also the result of government policy and not inherent in the free market.

Other than this, there would be no logical reason to assume that there is ever such a massive shortage of aggregate demand that the pessimism causes a large scale industrial shock. The individual relations between different producers of different goods do not change drastically and it would logically be that underinvestment should not be a problem. This is unless there was previously a period of overinvestment, but the keynesians usually deny that this happens[51]. If excessive investment results in the overuse of capital goods and the purchase of useless capital goods, we would see the goods that have been bought being abandoned. This is due to the fact that the investments into these capital goods turned out to not be profitable. Further forcing the use of the unprofitable and unproductive capital structures upon a society will result in a social loss of wealth.

And finally, the keynesians assume that the state can do anything to increase aggregate demand, this flies contrary to the nature of society and economics. The state can only shift resources from being occupied in one use at one time to be used at another use at another time, thus creating waste in the form of inefficient allocation of resources and the transaction costs of redistributing property titles. This means that the state can boost aggregate demand right now only at the cost of future aggregate demand, that

---

[51] For further information on this, I suggest reading various works on the Austrian Business Cycle theory. Especially the article "Austrian Busines Cycle Theory: A Brief Explanation" which is available on the website of the Mises Institute.

would create another crisis and only make everything worse. This is because the state has no productive power and can only rearrange resources, the state derives all resources from the population and doesn't create anything itself. Printing money does not increase economic value in a society and can only cause momentary overinvestment if it is thought that additional printed money is as valuable as previously printed money was. Even if the keynesians were right about everything else they could not in good faith propose that the state was the solution to aggregate demand gluts. The only way to ever actually escape a problem with aggregate demand is to shift more demand into the future in the form of saving. This goes contrary to what the keynesians believe that the solution is, only resulting in half-baked short-term solutions that take the economy from a crash to an even worse crash.

The final argument for why capitalism can't be sustained is that there is no way to facilitate indefinite growth from limited resources. At some point, capitalists must either get more resources or they must stop expanding and if capitalists stop expanding they become little more than parasites. If this is the case it would be true that capitalism could not be sustained and that we would need to give up the capitalistic system if we were to maintain an efficient economy. This argument seems logical on its face, it is true that capitalism expands and it is true that there are limited resources, thus it must be true that capitalism must stop expanding once these resources are put to use.

This relies on a very narrow interpretation of capital goods and natural resources. It is true that at some point we will run out of natural resources, but this does not mean that capitalism cannot expand further and that natural resources are the only capital goods. Even if there are no more resources we can still optimize the use of the resources we already have using the market economy, whether by repurposing them or substituting them. If we do that, we have another use of capitalism in sustaining our development even after natural resources are depleted and the system becomes oriented around preventing future losses. There can be profits from scarcity and there is no reason why we should not use capitalism to alleviate scarcity once there are no more natural resources to use.

The only way to prevent this scarcity is if we never used any natural resources at all, this is utopian at best. And I have seen no evidence that regulated systems offer better solutions for dealing with scarcity. Regulation can only enforce arbitrary restrictions on the optimization we see with the capitalist system, regulators don't need to make profits and as such don't need to look out for the best interest of anyone. They can just make popular moves and restrict the consumption of resources. Capitalists, on the other hand, need to maintain their profits and as such need to see that they can either utilize their resources in the future or find suitable substitutes for the resources that will be exhausted, it's simply not profitable to produce nothing. Thus capitalists will always find ways to be of service even if it's just by repurposing old goods or making the use of resources more efficient than it was before.

IV – Market Failure

There is a popular notion among economists that markets tend to fail occasionally in certain areas and as such, there is a role for the government to intervene in the economy insofar as to prevent these market failures from taking place. Market failure is defined as any outcome of the market where there is a conceivably better allocation of resources that at no cost makes someone else better off. This seems to make sense, when the market does not allocate resources in the most optimal way there has been a market failure and this has to be fixed. But when we look deeper into the logic of market failures we begin to unravel a misconception that nullifies the entire purpose for why we have markets instead of a centralized allocation of resources.

The first big thing is that capitalism is not only a profit based system but a profit and loss based system, this fundamentally means that any market failure will reflect as a lack of profit or an outright loss for the party who was responsible for the market failure. This makes it completely meaningless to act as if there should be any fix for market failures that is not endogenous in the capitalist system. The free market itself ensures that market failures will result in the persons who fail at properly allocating resources to experience personal failure. Capitalism internalizes both profits and losses when someone is responsible for a reduction in social wealth, they are forced to internalize the costs they imposed on others. Since these people experience personal failure due to their inability to allocate resources, it will result in a future better allocation of resources due to the signals caused by the misallocation of resources. Experiencing loss serves as a sign that the sort of behaviour should not be repeated in the future as to avoid allocating resources improperly. If it is said that resources are allocated improperly as they are allocated in an unpopular way, it ignores the fact that in the free market people are allowed to make unpopular decisions.

What is described as market failure is then simply the proper workings of the market and not some demonstrated mistake in the market, the entire reason to have markets is that mistakes reflect personally on the people who make them. Markets work perfectly when there is market failure. But then there are also the concerns with monopoly, externalities and the relationship between principal and agents[52]. I will be addressing externalities and the principal-agent problem here.

Externalities are not a clear-cut issue, but when we change our view of the market we must realize that the property rights that are necessary to facilitate the exchange of goods and services in a proper fashion require that all negative externalities are internalized. That is whenever something imposes a cost on someone that they did not want, if that person has a full right in their property, then that person should be able to contest the invasions of his property that caused the negative externality. There is also the question of negative externalities that do not strictly infringe upon the property of anyone, for example, a strip

---

[52] Monopolies and public goods are addressed in the following chapters.

club in a Christian neighbourhood. But these problems can be solved by voluntary action against those intrusions which will necessarily result in better outcomes than what the state could possibly offer. Externalities are not a problem even if they do not directly infringe upon other people's property. This holds true for any society, except the one where there is not even enough trust to establish commons in community management. This is unlikely in the real world.

There are also the questions of light and noise pollution, which we must also admit are violations of the property of people if they cannot fight the intrusive noise and the light. Excessive noise and light must be ceased if demanded by the owner of the property where the noise and light are being imposed upon. If they cannot be stopped in a reasonable manner, the owner of the property must be compensated for the intrusions caused by the noise and the light. And finally, there is the incredibly difficult issue of public decency when it comes to negative externalities. If people are committing lewd acts or anti-social acts in public, there is seemingly very little that anyone is able to do about it without the aid of the government. But to solve this we can just realize that when there is complete private property, there is no such public place where there are no controls over decency. The owners of roads and parks could simply exclude everyone who is acting in an indecent or annoying manner towards anyone else.

Thus the answer to negative externalities is not additional government but rather increased property rights for every party involved so they would not have to pay the costs for the actions of other persons. This also applies to environmental issues. When there are greater property rights allowed when it comes to the environment, large-scale pollution becomes impossible. Furthermore, the early preservation of scenic areas was advanced by railroad companies as they expected to profit from those who aimed to visit scenic areas. There are countless initiatives right now that aim to buy land to preserve and are only stopped by the government only allowing the sale of the resources in that land so as to deplete what the state-owned land has to offer. If there were greater property rights allowed in such areas of nature, then there would be no problems with pollution as the private owners of the land could combat the polluters who want to infringe on their property.

There are also positive externalities and it is supposedly inefficient to have these distributed among the entirety of society and as such there should be an internalization of these externalities. This makes absolutely no sense and is fundamentally absurd. When there are positive externalities, they exist only because all persons who have to pay the cost for the production of the externalities already benefit from the transactions they conduct. Any resulting byproduct in positive externalities is just a pleasant side effect. Furthermore, there is also the issue that every transaction results in positive externalities as they cause an additional abundance of goods which increases the purchasing power of money, to stop positive externalities is to stop a large factor of economic growth.

And finally, there is the principal-agent problem and other general asymmetric information problems, to understand the former we have to understand why the latter does not represent a failure in the market. Economists claim that when there is asymmetric information in which one party knows more than the other party, there is a problem in the market as people will make decisions that are less efficient than if they all knew as much as one another. But this is assuming that there is such a linear factor of knowledge in the market where some people simply have more or less knowledge and completely ignores very important informational features in the market. The first thing that is necessary to understand is that there is specialization required in the market and this applies to information, each person should know the most about his own area of expertise. This means that each person should know the most about the subjects that he himself earns money from as to be economically efficient and knowledge in other areas is less vital and thus should not be present if the opportunity cost is so high as to not be worth it.

This is because the amount of information a human brain can maintain is finite and there is no ability for each person to allocate the time to do thorough research about everything they consume. This means that asymmetric information is vital for the operation of the market as each person has to specialize in information if there is to be an efficient allocation of resources in the first place. This asymmetric information allows there to be a market, but supposedly the failure to guarantee equal information then leads to the ability of different parties to commit to trades that are not beneficial to them as they lack the information needed, but there are market solutions for this too. Whenever there is a significant enough purchase, people usually consult with specialists who have been trained to know and relay this information about that concrete purchase. When there are sufficiently small transactions people can simply learn from experience with barely any cost imposed on them. This is simply solved by the ordinary functions of the market and is not representative of the market failing.

The principal-agent problem is when some people use other people to further their own interest but both groups of people have different knowledge and interests. This creates a cost and inefficiency where the principal, who hires the agent, cannot directly know all the actions of the agent and has to provide the agent with incentives to do what the principal wants. This is an informational asymmetry that results in there being suboptimal results in the allocation of resources by the agent that goes contrary to the interests of the principal. But this is not a condemnation of the market and this problem is simply one that is representative of the failure in the corporate system and not a failure in the free market. This serves to demonstrate how large systems cannot function due to information problems and not how markets fail.

This is not a flaw in the market but rather the way in which any healthy market operates, complex informational structures with various tasks delegated and divorced from the persons who are ultimately responsible for the completion of those tasks should not be a desirable function of the market. To expect the free market to handle corporate structures is to expect the market to cater to inefficiency. The free market aims to maximize efficient behaviours wherever it is possible, thus corporate structures are disincentivized by the market. This is not a market failure but rather a demonstration for why corporations are unsustainable and why there are also problems with centralizing production. Most people already favour small businesses over large conglomerates, the free market will always tend to support small businesses. Whenever complex systems are centralized in such a way that the principal-agent problem becomes a relevant issue, the firm has already expanded beyond its own optimal size. It is important to realize that most of these large corporate structures are only even possible due to some incentives provided by the state. Thus the principal-agent relation is not a market failure but rather a guarantee that the market will not fail and will not cause additional centralization.

We need to also acknowledge that any method of economic allocation will have individual failures and that capitalism is the only system where individual failures cannot become systemic failures. When the government allocates resources, the government is even further divorced from the resources then any capitalist could ever be. This means that there is always an informational problem when it comes to the government. There are also problems with centralization or monopoly and negative externalities that are not internalized by the government as no one can force the government to internalize the negative externalities that it creates. The government is also the ultimate centralized agency as it holds all the power of violence in society. Thus the problems of monopoly will be extremely present when it comes to the government.

This means that the government will always be bound to fail and the agents within the government never learn anything from those failures as the income of the government is guaranteed. Taxation cannot be stopped by individuals unless there is a complete abolition of the current system of governance, the government can only lose revenue if the government itself becomes inefficient at collecting taxes or decides to spare people from taxation. Furthermore, the government has no interest in allocating the resources efficiently but rather has an interest in benefiting certain interest groups and not the population in general, this allows for the government to not even tend towards efficiency. Furthermore, government officials embody the greatest extent of the principal-agent problem. Every citizen should theoretically be the principal to every policeman, soldier, and bureaucrat. But most often the people hired by the government are not even somewhat accountable to the citizens whose functionaries they are supposed to be.

And this too applies to socialistic councils or other decentralized schemes, they too are not answers for market failure for most of the reasons the government is not. There will be government failure and socialist council failure in a much larger capacity than there is market failure, this is because market failure is represented in losses to the people whose resources are at stake. The market incentivizes increased efficiency in a manner that no other system of organization does.

V – Public Goods

Probably the most common defence of state involvement in the economy is the notion that there are some things that will be produced in lesser quantities than optimal if they are not produced by the government. This is the notion that we need the state to be involved so we can have a socially optimal number of police, military, roads and whatever other good that can be thought of as a public good. The explanation for this is simple, people would use some goods without paying and without causing damage and as such it will either be impossible or inefficient to provide these goods without the state. To be a public good something needs to meet two criteria, first, it has to be non-excludable, this means that it's impossible or extremely costly to exclude people from using that good. Secondly the good needs to be non-rivalrous, that means that a person using the good does not impose costs on the other people who use this good. If a good meets these two criteria then it is a public good.

There are multiple large issues with this logic. The first one is that all goods are rivalrous, there is no good which does not impose any additional costs upon using. If someone enters a near-empty bus, he may not cost the riders in immediate ticket money. But they cost the owner of the bus in uncompensated demand and thus indirectly raises ticket prices as the bus service itself needs to stay profitable. In this form, it is always costly to increase the number of people served without charging them as someone needs to pay for the raw materials and labour put into the people served.

Every good must be rivalrous. One can then make the distinction that it really is not a matter of cost but quantity, that a non-rivalrous good is one that does not reduce the quantity of the good left to others. However, this runs into the same issue, it may not directly reduce the quantity available to others to ride on that empty bus, but eventually, the bus needs to be repaired, fueled and driven. All of those cost money. To demonstrate this, if all but one person stopped paying for bus rides, that one person would have to cover the entirety of the cost and revenue of the bus.

The second point is that there is no optimal amount of goods other than that which is provided in accordance with the demonstrated preference of all individuals within an economy. People may think that they would be better off if they have more of some good, but are not willing to pay for it. This means that the tradeoff for some other good that could potentially be bought is not of enough value. This does not mean that the public is unable to decide how much of some good is necessary, but rather that the people calculating certain supposedly optimal amounts of spending on goods do not match the degree of spending people want in reality. We can now say that the political system may produce an excess of public goods, but this is better than producing a deficit, but we have to answer that the excess is at the expense of a deficit of some other good. It causes the same degree of inefficiency.

It's also widely popular to say that there could never be enough police or military when people would have to pay for these services, but we have to consider that the costs of police and military are not that great. In the vast majority of countries, police and military are not even a great minority of government spending and without taxation, we may even see more police and military, if anything. People are often driven to security over material indulgences. If we see a reduction in police and military we can only assume that these are unnecessary parts of the police and military as the people were not willing to demonstrate their preferences for these services.

And finally, all goods are non-excludable if we want to take that concept at face value without additional stipulations. When someone tries to use force to gain access to a good, it would make that good is as non-excludable as when someone violates property rights to gain access to a good. When roads and police are non-excludable we may say that your wallet is also non-excludable because a thief may steal it. We can then make the stipulation that all non-excludable goods are those goods which people can gain the same amount of value from without spending any money from simply the positive externalities. These are the services of the police and military which are supposedly of use to people who do not pay as they provide for general security.

But this is not true in war circumstances or in active conflicts, if you don't pay for police you may still live in a safer neighborhood and not get any help if you need it without exorbitant costs as momentary aid would be far more costly than a subscription, this will always happen for obvious reasons. There is also the concept of additional services provided by these institutions, right now there is no need for the police and military to provide value outside of conflicts, but there is a lot of utility in providing people with additional protections and access to resources if they pay more or at all. This could be in itself worthwhile enough that people actually pay into police and military for the additional benefits. For example, the police and the military could sell off used, yet functional weaponry that has been obsoleted at bargain prices. There are also empty facilities for the military and the police which could be used to aid those in need of the facilities. Forcing all services onto the market serves so as to make those services more valuable. This can create incentives to buy the services that are no longer offered by the state.

Furthermore, there would certainly be enough social pressure to push the people over the edge if those people think they can get away with not paying for defence. They may be fine with risking their lives if there's ever conflict and not getting access to services, but they will certainly be publicly shamed for not contributing to the police and the military as they get the positive externalities from those organizations. And even police and military aren't completely non-excludable by this definition, the externalities only apply to a very specific region, they can simply exclude any given region from their protection if not enough people are willing to pay for defence as providing defence would not be profitable. In the same way, the police of one state don't have to protect the people of another state, the police of one neighborhood might not have to protect the people of the next neighborhood over if they don't pay enough, thus becoming excludable to a much larger degree.

One may now bring up public utilities, sure, the public goods rhetoric does not hold up under scrutiny, but public utilities are still important and must be provided by a non-market entity and kept free for all. But there is no economic reason for why this should be the case, if these products are privatized, there may be some property disputes. But most problems can be worked out through market means as with any other service. We are only left with a moral case for why some services should be provided by the government or should be free. There is no real reason that the market cannot build the roads or the sewers.

The first moral case fails at every level, there is no conceivable upside for having something controlled by the government for the sake of it being controlled by the government. We may say that private companies may practice price gouging, but the government already does that much more than any private company could dream of. The government constantly spends way more money than necessary on projects that should be simple. Secondly, there is the incessant insistence that some goods should be controlled by the public as they are vital to everyday functioning. This logic would imply that all essential services ought to be controlled by the state. If you think that sewage and electricity need to be handled by the state, you also should think that the same applies to bread. The second moral case is that there needs to be a degree of equality in setting up the infrastructure for water and electricity and that people shouldn't have to pay more if they cost more to provide these services to. This also makes no sense, there is no need for those who live in accessible places where it's easy to bring pipes and electricity lines to subsidize those who live in inaccessible areas. There is no need to incentivize a move into areas in which it is harder to gain access to water and electricity and thus create larger costs for the rest of society.

The last possible argument that follows from logic related to the theory of public goods is that the government needs to provide some services for free as otherwise people would be left without essential services. Most of these claims are defeated by pointing out everything can be considered an essential service and thus people should either pay for most everything themselves or have the government pay for most everything. The final argument that can be derived from here is that some essential institutions, such as the police and courts need to be handled by one institution to avoid conflict and maintain social cohesion. Without all police being similar, everyone following one legal system, and these services being available freely to all, there would be chaos and a breakdown of society.

But this ignores that no one actually wants chaos and a breakdown of society and people will eventually have to solidify law systems and establish co-operative police systems. Functionally this will decentralize the systems of law and defence to the point where people can form communities around certain types of law, avoiding the problem altogether. And due to the digital age, this segregation does not even have to be physical, simply using digital tools can segregate people who may appear to be a part of one society. This is simply because people themselves want to avoid a breakdown of society and thus choose their own final arbiters and make sure that police are not killing each other.

As there is great market demand for stability, the market will provide stability.

VI – Monopoly

All people of all political affiliations fear one giant boogeyman in the capitalist economy, the monstrous monopolist who is able to escape the constraints of competition and charge massive amounts of money for products simply because there are no alternatives. This monopolist can undercut others when they try to develop alternatives and raise their prices again, doing maneuvers on the market that create unfair advantages upon unfair advantages. These nimble beasts pose every threat to the market economy and we need to avoid monopoly at any cost. At least this is what modern economic theory teaches so many of us.

To start off, I will address the hardest topic when it comes to monopoly, the topic of natural monopolies. These are industries with a large natural barrier to entry which are supposedly monopolized easily as new firms have a hard time entering these industries due to the great cost required to do so. Since there are these high natural barriers to entry, there are industries which need to be handled by the state to avoid the monopolization on the free market which would certainly happen with these industries. The most popular examples of these are roads, electricity, water, internet service providers and sewers.

These all require networks of land and as such are considered to have very large barriers to entry, although these functions can all be easily delegated to multiple smaller businesses. There is no need for local internet services to be joined to the larger internet grid by the same companies that provide the local internet. Other businesses may be responsible for larger grids, but local providers would be a completely viable strategy if it were not for the legal pressures by larger internet providers and regulatory burdens. Roads can similarly be split up into multiple smaller networks and integrated into larger wholes by the participants who benefit from the larger networks.

One can contend that this is inefficient or that people motivated by capitalist greed would not co-operate, but to do so is to ignore that access to larger networks increases the value of the services immensely and even though there could otherwise be "monopoly profits", the value of the service does not justify it. When smaller systems are integrated into larger wholes, they will be restricted by the guidelines of the larger wholes and unable to monopolize in such a fashion as they could if they were in control of the industry. This is because charging monopoly prices by any individual would lose value for everyone within the larger system.

There may be an objection that this is inefficient because it's hard to actually capture profits when the system is decentralized, but this is not true. There is no need for there to be giant toll booths at every junction if roads are privatized. This is especially in our digital age where collecting revenue can be handled without any friction with electronic solutions that are also extremely cheap. It would be easy to collect payment for the utility and it avoids the giant bureaucracies necessary for sustaining large ventures as each smaller venture can much more easily allocate their resources than a larger venture could. Thus forming a grid of road services, for example.

It can then said that there is a possibility of a cartel forming, but this ignores that cartels are volatile and unsustainable as they punish the most efficient firms since the cartels don't let them reduce prices to increase profits. In a collaborative venture, everyone benefits from a reduction of prices for any small unit. The cartel simply would not last if the road industry was cartelized. The same holds with the internet service providers, they could exploit their userbase in a grand manner, but that would require the full co-operation of all parties and that there is no other competition. This is unlikely as parties would then have a giant profit motive to try to find out how to compete with the antiquated system. Because of this, it is much better to have prices that are fair and not exploitative.

With water and electricity, it's a bit harder, they both require two parts of their infrastructure and that seems like a surefire way to get natural monopolies. They require a way to get access to a resource, whether it be collecting water or generating electricity and they then require a mechanism to distribute the resource that they generate. This seems like it would create immense costs as each person who wants to compete would have to set up their own water and electricity generation and then a giant grid, but this is not the case. Without the involvement of the state, it's most likely that the companies that produce clean water and electricity and those who distribute it are completely different. Furthermore, those who distribute water and electricity would probably not do so in large land areas but rather in locally concentrated areas where they can easily get all the benefits businesses get from decentralization in the form of information and the marginal benefits of conforming to the optimal size of the industry.

And finally the problem of sewage, a lot of people claim that sewage is simply not profitable for some reason, but that's unfounded, people are willing to pay a lot of money to not have to deal with their own filth. If the sewage system can get rid of this filth, it can earn great revenues by charging what the market allows it to charge. And the sewage can be converted into products such as fertilizer and clean water, with a market incentive to do this, these processes would certainly be much more effective than they are right now.

Another reason why people think all of these are natural monopolies is because they don't understand competition and what it entails and assume that all competition is overlapping. In actuality we can separate competition into three large parts, all to do with the choices consumers can make. First there is the overlapping competition, theoretically, everything is in overlapping competition with each other good as each good requires the forfeiture of other goods. But most often this is understood as between goods that are easily substitutable with one another. Overlapping competition is the competition that happens directly with different companies outbidding each other. With natural monopolies, this overlapping competition is barely relevant as they are industries in which this is not efficient.

There is also potential competition, this is the chance that in the future your company will experience monetary losses due to the actions of another company. This is why companies sometimes take long-term approaches where they sell products in such a manner that may not be as efficient in the moment as they can be, but in the long term will benefit greatly from the prudence they showed. The only situation where "predatory pricing" is practised is the situation in which current low prices can facilitate future low prices. This is why some companies opt to take losses in the present to establish a better market position in the future. It is not an example of monopolization, but rather of healthy competition. Companies are forced to lower their costs due to the potential of competition as they would be when there was overlapping competition. With natural monopolies, potential competition is too barely relevant as the costs to entry are fairly high. Because of this, it may seem like when any industry needs large infrastructure it will become noncompetitive and be a monopoly.

This logic ignores parallel competition, when the competition is not overlapping and when the competition is not potential. This may be fairly hard to understand but we can simply look at it as the pressure to modernize due to the quality of other industries around the current industry and the competition created by the value of the land in different areas. When some grid system is outdated in one place, there can be an improved water system being built in another place. When the current system of managing water is outdated and expensive, the value of land decreases as the services are comparatively worse than they were before. Since the areas around are modernizing, there is pressure for the natural monopoly to too improve its services rather than offer nothing and expect a high amount of customers.

This only works on the level of cities with the state economy where the entire grid is managed by one entity, but if the grid system was decentralized and if each person involved could simply request a connection to the grid a few hundred feet over, which would result in moving grids without physically moving, there would be a tremendous amount of pressure for the existing grids to improve their services. In reality, we see an example of this with different counties and their school systems, even though this is not market competition, it serves to demonstrate how "monopolies" of this sort can compete. In many areas, the local government invests in the schools to attract more people to their area and it often works. People move to places where their children can get a proper education, even though the school system is monopolized by each local government, there is some degree of pressure to modernize due to this.

Parallel competition may not be as effective as the other types of competition in lowering prices or improving quality, but it still does not allow any one business to hold a natural monopoly. The fact that there is a high barrier of entry into a business does not mean that it is necessarily inefficient or that there can be no competition due to the high barrier to entry. And we still have to realize that potential competition and overlapping competition still take place to a smaller degree, no matter how much some industry is a natural monopoly. Competition is a dynamic process and not something that can be simply measured by just counting the number of businesses, and even if we count the number of businesses that operate on a market, we may consider that the monopolistic actions may be due to the state.

And as a final note with natural monopoly, there are claims that there is an excessive duplication of resources that would otherwise not be there if the entire industry was controlled by a singular entity. There may be places where there are two water lines instead of one, which would be a tremendous waste. Funnily enough, almost no one claims that it's a tremendous waste to have different types of bread at the supermarket and that it's a terrible thing when the bookstore sells more than one book, as creating additional books is terribly inefficient and should not take place. The entire reason we think of multiple grid systems in one area as a terrible waste is because of how difficult it is currently to establish grid systems due to the government managing resources. We can imagine an integrated system of below ground tunnels which could make it easy for any person to establish their own grid system with only having to rent the tunnel space from the person who owns that tunnel. The government does nothing like this and we can't expect that doing nothing is the only right thing to do in this scenario, there could be much more competition if all areas were subject to the profit motive and not to bureaucratic control.

Even though natural monopoly is the most difficult topic to address, there are still other fears of monopoly that people constantly point towards when it is said that the market should be free. Without the government to get rid of big businesses that have grown beyond some arbitrary measure of size, we would have industries controlled by singular entities and not by competitive entities that increase quality and lower costs. To demonstrate this, most people point towards the gilded age to show how terrible it was when the government did not control monopolization and how the robber barons monopolized industry and made giant profits without doing anything better than otherwise would have been done.

But there are two giant misunderstandings when it comes to this, first in the gilded age and whenever there are these giant monopolies there has never been a stop in improving quality. This is because large operations can improve quality tremendously, but only when lead by incredibly apt leaders who can economize the resources that they manage. And this is historically demonstrated with the industries that were monopolized in the gilded age basically always exhibiting falling prices rather than increasing prices. This makes the entire theory of monopoly seem absurd and it's because it ignores two important aspects of market competition. Every good is to a degree substitutable with any other good. This means that the choice is not only between two different brands of gasoline but also between gasoline and fish. One may decide to forgo the purchase of gasoline to purchase some fish, this ensures that there is always a reason to decrease prices no matter how uncompetitive any certain industry is.

The second part is that large businesses are inherently inefficient as they have a degree of personal disengagement between different levels. It's also much harder to calculate how much money needs to go to what purposes when the different levels of the business cannot use market signals to determine resource allocation in the same way as they could if they outsourced the way in which they distribute resources. And the only way a business can get large on a perfectly free market is if it can manage to be so much more efficient than the original competition. This means that monopolies when they are monopolies need to constantly remain at peak efficiency as everything is against them when it comes to internal structure.

The monopoly may hold a strong market position, but it is inherently unstable as the different parts of the business have thousands of needs and it is impossible to calculate rationally how much money needs to go to which part of the business. To illustrate this, we may take the example of a large burger chain. In an individual restaurant, the cook needs to have the materials for burgers and he needs to prepare these in accordance with the demand. This is where market calculation can take place perfectly, when a customer places his order, the cook fills the order. However, the manager of the restaurant needs to order supplies for the cooks, since the cook cannot get the supplies to exact needs, it must be ensured that there is neither a great shortage of materials or a great excess of materials. Both create waste.

And with most restaurants, there is already waste as the process of cooking is divorced from the process of managing, if there was a way to instantly co-operate between the restaurant cooks and those who sell the materials there would be no such waste. But this has its own problems and in the vast majority of the cases, having a manager is better than no manager as the expertise can overall increase efficiency in the long term and allocate resources more rationally. With large enterprises there are tens of levels in the corporate structure, all experiencing this degree of divorce between the different levels and all having this inherent waste[53].

For these reasons, there is no rational fear of monopolies that manage to be inefficient because they are monopolies, the corporate structure of any large business is extremely fragile as it is and this means that there is no room for inefficiency in large enterprises on a completely free market. There is also no room for corporations, as they require having a legal barrier from responsibility. This same logic applies to any and all cartels, except each member of the cartel also has an incentive to lower their prices to ensure that they have more profits, which leads to the eventual collapse of every cartel.

The only response to this is the notion of predatory pricing, that monopolies can leverage their greater market position to eliminate competition by having their prices be below their costs and when competition is gone, raising prices again. But this has never happened in the history of economics and for a good reason, there is still competition. It has happened that companies lower their prices below cost, but in that case, this is just the healthy manifestation of competition as consumers get to experience lower prices. And since this is unsustainable, other businesses can easily resume competition once these ventures have finished their predatory pricing and the market position has been leveraged to the fullest potential. This results in the transaction of wealth from the

---

[53] This is partially solved by having a system of franchise where individual entrepreneurs are able to start brand restaurants.

business to the consumer The other businesses in the economy also have the ability to buy the goods the company is selling below cost with the intention to resale them in the future. Since the predatory pricing is unsustainable, hoarding cheaper goods seems like a prudent decision to make. There is no economic logic that can properly explain why predatory pricing is actually a significant threat.

We still have to explain why monopolies even exist if they are inefficient. The answer is fairly simple, monopolies can exert power over the state securing their market position using the state to prevent competition. This can be done with increasing barriers to entry artificially with regulation and licensing or by creating special privileges for certain corporations that allow them to flourish while others have to pay the costs. Every monopoly in the history of economics that has raised prices and reduced quality has been propped up by the government.

The economic concept of monopoly even originated from the notion of the government giving out exclusive licenses, the association of competition on the free market and monopoly is a very recent one and not something that has existed for a significant amount of time. This has resulted in a combination of early monopoly theory that criticizes exclusive licenses by the government and modern theory that considers every business that holds a dominant market position a monopoly. The two sets of logic do not match up as they come from wholly different premises. We must oppose monopolies as exclusive licenses that shield businesses from competition, but on the free market, no business is shielded from this competition even if they are the only business in their industry.

Capitalism Works
by Insula Qui

©2018 Insula Qui
No Rights Reserved

Author: Insula Qui
Contact: insulaqui@gmail.com

The author of this book hereby waives all claim of copyright (economic and moral) in this work and immediately places it in the public domain; it may be used, distorted or destroyed in any manner whatsoever without further attribution or notice to the creator.

www.ingramcontent.com/pod-product-compliance
Lightning Source LLC
Chambersburg PA
CBHW031610210526
45464CB00004B/1506